THE STRAITS
IMPREGNABLE

THE STRAITS IMPREGNABLE

BY SYDNEY DE LOGHE

The Naval & Military Press Ltd

Published and © by the
The Naval & Military Press

Unit 10 Ridgewood Industrial Park,
Uckfield, East Sussex, TN22 5QE
Tel: +44 (0) 1825 749494
Fax: +44 (0) 1825 765701

TO

THE FIRST AUSTRALIAN DIVISION

This Book,
Written in Australia, Egypt and Gallipoli,
is true.

CONTENTS

THE STRAITS IMPREGNABLE

CHAPTER I

THE CALL

THE afternoon was wearing out, and I began to think of home and tea. I stopped working, straightened my back, ran moist fingers through my hair, and sat down on the log. The axe went tumbling to the ground. "Watch-and-pray" and "Wait-and-see" got up from the fallen gum suckers, and trotted forward with waving tails and glistening, slippery tongues. I made haste to get rid of them. They began to play, biting ears and growling, but went back at last, laid keen black heads on narrow paws and watched me out of grave brown eyes.

To Gippsland spring had come. The day had been a day of spring until evening beckoned afternoon away. Now a little breeze—gentle, but rather cold—came out of the west and wandered through the tops of the gum suckers. The scent of eucalyptus came with it; and behind it followed the voices of countless rustling leaves.

It moved among the wattle tops where they wound along the river; it moved across the rape crops and over the grassy flats beyond. It bent the sedges in the lagoons where the first black ducks were feeding, and where, on warmer nights, big eels bubbled below the sunken logs. I raised my forehead to the cool; and, lo! the breeze had gone!

Through the rape crop sheep were streaming. Anxious ewes pulled hurriedly at the broad green leaves or watched with care their frolicking youngsters. On the flats, round the salt trough, the bullocks chewed and meditated. Smoke climbed up by the river bend; and outside her cottage moved Mrs. Pigg, bringing in the washing, pulling vegetables, feeding the fowls. Small and busy the distance showed her.

Behind me, and on either side, the suckers pushed up their heads. High over them leaned spectral trees: blackened, leafless, stripped of bark, weary with long waiting. About the ground great trees had fallen: grim logs—knotted logs—logs scarred with the breath of summer fires. Here and there showed feeding sheep; and this way and that way ran well-worn pads leading to the waterholes in the wattles. Over the hillside spread a faint green carpet where was shooting the young grass.

Out from hidden gullies floated cries of sheep. Mournfully they travelled across the hillside—now the voice of a ewe whose lamb had strayed, now a lamb hungry and alone. Other sights and sounds began to fill the evening. Small finches came hopping into the suckers, dodging and peeping and swinging through the boughs, and preening themselves between the leaves. Gay was the twittering as the hunt for supper went forward. Then a jackass swooped into a tree top, threw up tail, raised high head and pealed out frenzied laughter. Other tree tops joined the madman chorus. Next a magpie hopped upon the big log and glinted an evil eye at me; and then forgot me to ruffle sombre shoulders, and join the evening hymn.

The sun was on the horizon, and shadows moved quickly across the lower lands. First they filled the reedy lagoons, the big wattle groves, the belts of scrub. They moved from bramble bush to grass tussock, from fallen log to waterhole. Faint wisps of fog rose about the river. It was late; I was hungry; it was time for home.

I put out a hand for my coat, picking up the axe as well; and "Watch-and-pray" and "Wait-and-see" sprang forward with glad barks. I pushed them off and got up.

"Hullo there, Guv'nor," a harsh voice shouted from the ruined gate, and old Scottie came through the gap on his ancient chestnut mare. The long sunbeams shone upon his weather-beaten face, with its broken yellow teeth and small hard beard. He wore an ulster, with a sugar-bag hanging out of the pocket. In the bag he had dived a horny hand, and now it came out filled with letters and papers. "Here you are, Guv'nor," he shouted again.

I went forward and took the packet, picking

out all that belonged to me. What was left I handed back. "There are one or two for the Piggs," I said. "You might take them over."

"Right-o, sir," he answered, and pulled the old mare round, and started away at a jog-trot. Through the suckers man and beast disappeared —an elderly man and a very elderly beast.

I leaned against the gateway and opened the letters. There was news from home, telling of weather five weeks old, and a garden party older yet. Still I read it all twice. An agent had written of some bullocks, and there was a third note about sheep. I pushed everything into my coat pocket, and picked up the papers. Four were there—I had not been to the township for a day or two. I opened the oldest of them, dated four days ago, and turned the pages in a hurry —I was hungry and thinking of tea.

But I forgot tea. Across the middle leaves ran staring headlines. Austria was at the throat of Servia, and war was a matter of hours. All Europe was arming.

I opened another paper. Events had gone forward. Austria had begun the journey of chastisement. From East to West of Europe sounded the clamour of war. I scanned the pages, and threw the paper down. The next I opened, and again the next. No line of hope!

I leaned and read.

Dusk was deepening, and slow grey fogs wended across the flats. "Watch-and-pray" and "Wait-and-see" sat erect upon their haunches, peering up to know why I delayed. The evening had grown still again, birds and sheep alike were silent; but from the Piggs' cottage smoke climbed in cheerful wreaths. Pigg and his wife were at tea now, old Scottie no doubt with them: they were talking of war and ruin, though half a world lay between.

I picked up the fallen papers and put the axe upon my shoulder. "Here, 'Watch-and-pray,' here, 'Wait-and-see,' we're off at last!" I took the path through the ti-tree, though it was boggy still from the rains, and brought the dogs to heel as we passed beside the river through flocks of dozing sheep. Out of the calm skies first stars were coming. We reached the cattle-yards, and pushed a way through the loose barbed wire. The breath of honeysuckle was blown from Scottie's cottage, but the place was dark and empty. Scottie had not come back.

We left the yards to go along the path which crossed the hillside; then dipped into the gully and climbed the opposite bank. The horses stood under the pepper trees in a lazy, drowsy circle. I glanced into the buggy-shed to see that all was secure. I pulled open the garden gate. It was evening now, full evening, grey and a trifle chill; and among the grasses crickets shrilled and from the waterhole by the lightwood tree rose the voices of amorous frogs.

A score of perfumes met me at the garden gate. The peaches, pears, and apples were a-flower; and the lemon trees and oranges budded. When we came to the house, I reached down the dogs' meat from the shelf beside the window, and led the way to the kennels, which were among piles below the flooring. The dogs began to bark again, and ran to their places, sitting down to be chained up. I chained them, gave them their meat and a goodnight pat, and went round to the back once more.

The house key came from its hiding-place, and I unlocked the door and went inside. In the kitchen it was nearly dark: in the front room it was darker; but there were matches by the lamp on the table. Then I opened the front door and went on to the verandah. Roses had climbed all above it, all round it, all across it; and on either side the flowering peaches leaned for support. I pushed aside the rose branches and stepped down into the garden. The stars were shining and, across the creek, lights had come out in every farmhouse. The milking was over at the Browns', for a drowsy stream of cows returned to the paddock. I watched them a moment, and next went to the back of the house again. At the woodheap I picked up an armful of sticks to carry into the front room. Quite soon the fire was started, and it burned brightly. Then forwards and backwards I went into the kitchen, bringing the kettle to put on to the fire, carrying in plates and knives and forks, bread, butter. The table laid, out I went to the woodheap again, and this time chopped big logs. In the chill evening the axe blows sounded sharp and clear. It meant three journeys to the front room with the logs; but those made, I was ready for the night.

I took off boots and leggings, throwing the spurs into the corner. I went into the bedroom and washed, splashing water all over the place. Then I found the frying-pan and lard, and began a dish of eggs and bacon. The kettle boiled for the tea. Soon the bacon was cooked and the eggs were ready; all was there, and the fire shining. I drew in a chair and began to eat. Presently out of a pocket the papers came, one by one to be read through. Long after I had finished eating, by the light of the lamp and the fire I sat reading on.

At last I got up. A kettle of water boiled, and I carried into the kitchen the supper things and washed up. In ten minutes the business was over. I made the bed ready, and put more wood on the fire. By this time it was eight o'clock. For a moment I waited by the mantelpiece, looking into the flames; but they were too hot, and drove me on to the verandah. Once more the perfume of countless blossoms met me in the dark.

There was no moon; it was all starlight, and on the right hand the Southern Cross swung round. At the garden end, the big waterhole glimmered through gaps in a broken fence, and from it came love-songs of a thousand frogs, while in the overhanging branches of the lightwood two cranes kept mournful watch. Each night they stood there at this hour, peering down into the reeds below.

The hill climbed up behind the house and fell away before me. All over it tall, barkless trees stood up—grimly some, some wearily—but each one a spectator of the endless procession of day and night. Across the ground other trees were lying. Bracken had closed round some and brambles had clambered over others. I heard the rippling of the river, and here and there caught the gleaming of waters: there beside the great white gums, there below the willows, there before the bridge; and farther off, upon the plains, showed there and there the farmhouse lights. Round all ran the distant hills. Now from afar a dog barked, now a bull bellowed; and ever, ever shrilled and croaked the crickets and the frogs.

The evening was cold enough for an overcoat, and, putting one on, I sat down on the verandah step. Most nights this was my custom before turning into bed. On and off, for two years, I had come out in the same way—on starry nights, on moonlit nights; on nights of cloud, on nights of rain; on nights of mist, of warmth, of cold. I had lain back on stifling nights when the mosquito alone seemed abroad; and I had felt the breath of the frost come down and had fled beaten to the fireside. For two years I had watched the seasons come and go, and the stars swing round and round. Not a night but I could tell when the moon would sail up behind the hills. I had seen suns set in the West—and I had watched and watched until the East grew rosy.

Two years had I owned and lived upon these lands. I had challenged the wilderness, driving it ever back. I had known days of hope and days of uncertainty; but victory was within sight. Where scrub had waved, now was open country; where logs mouldered, now passed the plough. The fight had cost two years—but I had won.

Over the silent meadowlands I looked, where rape and oats were growing. "Two years have you spent here," they seemed to say, "and this third year is to be the year of your hopes. We shall repay your labours; wait but a while."

I looked to the gap in the hills where the moon would climb forth, moving and mounting, presently to sail over lands where stalked sorrow and desolation.

A voice asked, "Will you stay here for your payment? Or will you leave it—to follow the moon?"

"Aye, but why should I follow the moon?" said I. "What hate have I to take me there? No; hard have I toiled; let me remain."

"Stay with your plough, then," said the voice. "Muster your cattle and count your sheep. But never more shall you dwell alone. A stranger shall sit in your heart. A stranger shall abide with you to taunt you of your choice."

The dogs woke me up. Footsteps came slowly along the path behind the house, and old Scottie went by on his way across the hill. Crowbar, shovel, and axe were on his back, and laden thus he passed away into the gloom of trees and suckers.

Through the wet winter we had pulled together fallen logs for burning; and before a giant heap Scottie stopped, and laid down tools. He rested a moment on the pile, to get breath no doubt; but quite soon started a search among the standing trees and bracken. He was looking for kindling. It was so dark—often I could not follow him. Presently he was back again at the heap; and a tender flame crept up, changing gloom into fairyland. An army of shadows were born, and leaped about the magic circle. Old Scottie was plainly now to be seen, even his stumpy beard; and the axe flashed when the flames danced on the blade.

The light grew broader and bolder, and flames licked through the gathered logs, while on all sides moved Scottie, like a priest at the altar—chopping, levering, and digging with axe, crowbar, or shovel. Now he would hurry away with burning sticks to another pile, so that furnaces grew out of half the hillside. With each breeze crossing the river, flames leaped and logs roared; and flights of sparks raced up into the night. The smoke coils were caught to the treetops, and the lofty, leafy boughs, drawn into the maelstrom, were dashed about. From furnace to furnace passed Scottie, tending their needs as a doctor watches his patients.

The night was ageing; all but one farmhouse light had gone out; but I did not think of sleep. I realised the cold and, rising, went inside. The fire still burned. The alarm clock on the mantelpiece said a quarter past ten. I went into the kitchen in search of cake, and next passed through the back door into the open, and took the track cut in the hillside, the track Scottie had taken. While I followed it, the light at the Smithsons' disappeared. As I came up, Scottie peered at me through the smoke.

"Hallo, Guv'nor," he shouted. Then he shouted again, waving a hand at the fires, "They're going well! Have you come to help? It wull take two tae shift some of these!"

I nodded. He picked up the crowbar, I bent down for the shovel; and for the next hour we made the rounds. By that time all the fires had taken good hold and could be left until morning. We were hot, dry, and tired, and with one accord found seats on a log. I crossed hands on the shovel handle, laid my chin on them, and thus fell to watching the fog bands form over the river. I was surprised Scottie was so quiet: he stopped talking so seldom. Now he was content to spit and fill his pipe. This filling was slow of completion and only ended when he had blown and coughed and gurgled through the pipe stem.

"Guv'nor," he said presently, and I stopped watching the river and looked round, "the papers say there wull be a lot doing at home. We wull be fighting Germany in a day or two. Don't you say so, Guv'nor?"

"Yes," I answered.

He smoked on, pressing a finger into the bowl of his pipe. "If it's a big thing, men wull go frae this country. Don't you think so?"

"I expect so," I said.

He cocked his head on one side. "Maybe one or two frae down here wull be going."

"I shall be going," said I.

CHAPTER II

ENLISTED

NEARLY a month afterwards Ted was driving me to the camp.

The wind had worked up into half a gale, and much of the way clouds of dust swept into our faces. The ponies faced the weather unwillingly, and Ted did not spare the whip. I crouched back in the buggy, with hat hard over my eyes, and for minutes together neither of us said a word, unless it was to curse our luck. Sometimes the gale dropped, the dust lay down, the sun shone again; and then we found ourselves in grassy country, hilly and also flat. Up once more jumped the wind, and the dust sprang after it. It was damnable, nothing less.

At last, at a level crossing, we turned sharply to the right, and the buggy hood afforded some shelter. Between the dust storms, the camp was to be seen, ahead and to the left hand. Tents stretched over many acres. Also I caught a glimpse of paddocks filled with manœuvring infantry and occasional artillery teams. Then we were passing a long row of pines. Opposite them were open paddocks, with Melbourne in the distance.

"It'll be somewhere about here," Ted said, moving his head my way, and he pulled the horses into a slow trot.

The road began to fill up. Half-companies of infantry passed us in an opposite direction, made up of uniformed men and men in civilian dress. The whole moved to the shouts of sergeants and lesser fry. A gun team and ammunition waggon rumbled by. The horses were awkward, the harness stiff, the drivers at sea. A mounted N.C.O. called the wrath of Heaven on the whole affair. We steadied to a walk, and the team ambled past.

"This must be the place," Ted said again, and stopped the ponies. I pushed my head round the buggy hood to find us at an opening in the fence, with a sentry on guard there. The other side of the fence was a paddock filled with tents in rows, and between each row ran horse-lines. Between the tents and the road were drawn up guns and ammunition waggons.

"Yes, this must be the place."

Ted drew into the footpath while I got out. "I'll wait somewhere about here," he said, moving up on the road at a walk and calling back.

The sentry challenged me; but my pass let me in. I asked for the Colonel, and was directed straight ahead. Inside the lines, much was going on. Men ran, trotted, and walked; joked, argued, and shouted. Tents were going up, horses were being picketed; things were topsy-turvy. And of uniform, some men possessed military hats only, others had on military shirts, others military breeches; but the majority wore their civilian clothes. Busy men were to be seen; but just as many loafed round. Outside the quartermaster's store, equipment of every sort was piled: all painfully new. A score of men lingered round it, and there seemed to be four or five unwilling sorters. In the middle stood the Q.M. with store lists in his hands.

I passed up a line of tents with horses picketed on the left hand, and at the top asked the way again of an individual balancing himself on a tentpeg. He pointed to a large tent not far away, and stared hard after me when I left him.

Outside the big tent was a notice—HEADQUARTERS FIELD ARTILLERY BRIGADE. An orderly stood in the doorway, lighting a cigarette. Him I asked for the Colonel. "D'you want him?" the orderly said. He pushed up the flap of the tent. I stooped and went in. The tent was furnished with a table and several chairs; at the table three officers sat. Table and chairs were covered with papers and books, and all three men were writing. Round the walls stood packing cases, filled to overflow with strange instruments, odds and ends of harness, and signalling flags. I came to a full stop.

Two of the men went on with their work, but the third—the youngest of them, a lieutenant about twenty—looked up, eyed me, and yawned. When he had finished, he picked up pen again, and remarked casually: "What do you want?"

When he spoke, the other men stopped writing and lifted their heads.

The centre man was a big man, and by cap and shoulder strap I knew him as the Colonel. The third man was small and sharp featured, by rank Captain—the Adjutant, I guessed.

"I would like to see Colonel Jackson," said I.

The big man put down pen. "I am Colonel Jackson."

I looked him over as he spoke. He was a middle-aged man—nearly fifty, I thought, and rather handsome. His hair was turning grey, his complexion was high, and I warrant he knew how to enjoy life. He looked me straight in the face. A good soldier, I thought: a man worth following. The Captain started writing, and only paused from time to time to run a pen through his close-clipped moustache.

"Yesterday I received notice from the Commandant at Victoria Barracks to report to you," I began. "I volunteered, and have passed the medical examination."

"What is your name?"

"Lake."

"Have you had any military training?"

"I am sorry, none; but I can ride and shoot." And I added, "I hope this won't stand in my way. I am very anxious to get in."

The Colonel drummed his fingers on the table a moment or two, and all the while looked at me. In the end he spoke gravely.

"You know, Lake, a soldier's life is a hard life, a very hard life—bad food, the ground for a bed, exposure to all weathers, work all hours. The officer is no better off than the man."

"I have not rushed into it," I said. "I have thought it over and hope you will take me." To this he answered nothing. "I have some horses," I went on, "which would suit a gun team. I shall be glad to give them if they are of any use."

He misunderstood me. "Oh," he said, "we have enough now. In any case the Government does not give a high price. What do you want for them?"

"I don't want to sell," I said. "I make an offer of them. They are plough horses, and, should I go away, I shall not plough this year. I am glad to offer them."

"Lake, I don't think there is any need for that. As long as a man gives his own services, it is all that can be expected. Keep your horses. If you join, when can you come into camp?"

"I can come now; but I should like first to go back to Gippsland. I have a place there."

"That can be arranged." He turned to the lieutenant who first had spoken to me. "Sands, take Lake to the doctor and afterwards swear him in."

I noticed Sands got up rather hurriedly when the Colonel's eye reached him; but he recovered himself outside the tent. He pushed his hat on to the back of his head, stuffed both hands in his pockets and led the way all over the place. The doctor was not in his tent and seemed to have died or deserted. We wandered about endlessly, without any obvious plan of campaign. Now and then Sands would stop some one and ask when the doctor had last been seen; and always he finished by swearing in a bored kind of way. Then off we moved again.

At last we found ourselves where we had started —outside the big tent. "Stay there," Sands said suddenly, and disappeared inside. He came out with a large printed paper, a book, a pen, and a bottle of ink. The bottle of ink he balanced on a post, the pen he put between his teeth. Next he began to open out the sheet; and the wind took hold of it, shook it and wrestled with it; and he bungled it, crumpled it, and finished by swearing again. But in the end he won, and we took up opposite positions and made a start on our business. He asked endless questions, which I answered, and we came to the oath. "Take off your hat," he said. He became solemn in a moment with an ease entirely his own and took off his hat. Next he held out a Bible. I took it and we began the oath. The wind blew, Sands mumbled; and there was difficulty in following what he said. More than once he eyed me sternly, and repeated the sentence. But we came through it safely, the signatures were made, the ceremony was ended. There was still the doctor's signature to get; but Sands was sick of me. He pushed the paper into my hand, waved in the direction of the doctor's tent, and departed.

I journeyed anew after the doctor, and this time found him in his tent. He was alone, reading a long letter and smiling over it. He asked what

I wanted, told me to strip, and went on reading. He read still when I was ready; but presently put the letter away and started to tap me. He tried my teeth, tried my eyes, said I would do, and, while I dressed, filled in the papers.

I took the papers to the Brigade Office, and gave them to Sands. The Colonel was there, talking to an officer I did not know. "Captain Knight, I am giving Lake to you," he said. "He will be coming on Sunday or Monday; in the meantime he is going down to Gippsland. Make him out a railway pass, will you?"

The captain swung round. He was a clean, rather well dressed man, with a restless manner. "Yes, sir," he said, saluting. He told me to follow him, and marched off down a row of tents and across horse-lines, until we came to a tent with a notice board in front. A sergeant-major and a couple of clerks were inside writing: sundry other fellows hung round the door. Knight bounced into the tent with me at his heels.

"This man has been given to us, sergeant-major. He wants to get down to Gippsland to-morrow. Make a pass out, please." He turned to me. "When can you come, Lake?"

"Sunday or Monday," I answered.

"Then come here Sunday morning. We have not much time, and you ought to get in all the drills you can. I can't wait. The sergeant-major will give you your pass." He went off at full speed.

I was given the railway pass, and left the tent with mixed feelings. There was no drawing back;

but—yes—I was glad. I walked fast, guessing Ted would be bored, and in truth he was at the gate, passing time by cracking his whip.

"I'm in!" I called out. Ted grinned and drew the reins together.

Next day I went home for the last time. Ted was with me, and we drove in a hired buggy the eight miles from the station. Scottie, who burnt off near the road, met us at the gate. The sun was shining; the day was very mild.

We had come over long, rutty roads with scarcely a word spoken between us, and when Scottie opened the double gates we turned in with as little remark, following at a walk the track to the house. Here and there stood up thick patches of hoary bracken; and charred logs lay this way and that way to bar the path. While the plough lay idle, Scottie and I had thinned and trimmed the wilderness on the hillside; but much still remained to be done. At it I looked and said: "This is my last day here. When I return, this will be clean and green with grass. I shall be glad; but I shall remember affectionately times which have gone."

Soon we were at the house. The dogs jumped at their chains and greeted us frantically, so that I stepped down from the buggy and for the last time set them free. We unharnessed the horses, taking them to the yards behind the buggy shed; and while I stooped to pat the dogs, Ted walked a few paces away, spread apart his legs, took off his hat, and scratched slowly the centre of his head. I pushed aside the dogs and got up.

"You have a look over the place," I called out, "and I'll fix up things inside. If I finish in time, I'll come and look for you; otherwise you'll find me here."

He nodded in a dreamy way, and went on scratching his head. When finally he came out of the brown study, it was to wander off at a snail's pace towards the La Trobe flats. I had waited by the garden gate for him to say something, but he went off without a word and I made for indoors.

I threw open the kitchen door, the sitting-room door, the bedroom door, the front door, and the sunlight tumbled into the house. Hat and coat went on to the table, and that was all the ceremony before business. Out came every drawer and open came every box; and in a heap on the floor fell papers and old letters. One or two bills which turned up I filed; all else travelled to the fireplace, where match and poker were sole mourners at the funeral. It took time, for I was thorough, and in the end it was too late to look for Ted. Instead, I went on to the verandah and sat down on the step, looking towards the river. The sun shone over the paddocks; but the afternoon had grown cooler.

There was little or no wind, so that things had become very still. A few birds whistled to one another in the trees behind the house; but the sheep were camped out of sight on the flats, and the bullocks fed in the scrub far away. Across the river, small figures moved to and fro. The Browns cut chaff by the willows, the Smithsons mended a fence by their cultivation. Over the hilltop, down the road, ran children home from school.

"Thus it was yesterday," I said, "thus will it be to-morrow, but I shall not look on. I watch this for the last time. My kingdom is passing into other hands. A stranger will sit at the fire at night. A stranger will read my books. A stranger will watch the rabbit-fence, will count the cattle and muster the sheep. A stranger will hear the parrots whistling, the jackass laughing, the magpie jodeling. A stranger will see the floods rise and fall, will feel the heat of summer and winter's bitter grip. A stranger will mark the changing seasons and count the stars sailing through the skies. Round and round Time's wheel will go. So be it."

After half an hour Ted wandered back. I chained the dogs up, kneeling to say a long goodbye to them. Maybe they understood, for they barked and scratched and jumped wildly. We put the horses in the buggy, and in climbed Ted and I climbed after him. He picked up the reins and flicked the whip across their shoulders, moving them forward at a walk. There we were, following for the last time the track to the gate. Behind us the dogs were crying.

Old Scottie waited at the gate to give me a dirty hand.

"Goodbye, Guv'nor," he said. "Come back again."

"Goodbye, and good luck, Scottie. Look after things," I answered.

That done, we were through the gate, rattling down the road. Beyond the rabbit-fence the sheep in the rape gazed up with stupid eyes; a turn, and we were beneath the gums spreading vast arms above the river; another turn, and we bumped over the wooden bridge, where dead wattle blossoms fell upon us. Then I looked back for the last time—and next the trees came between.

CHAPTER III

TRAINING

At the camp gate I said goodbye to Ted, and he promised to look me up in a day or two, or as soon as he could. We made no heart-breaking affair of the ceremony, and before I was inside the gate the ponies moved in an opposite direction. I saw Ted touch them with the whip to get them into their collars, then the buggy hood hid him and I saw him no more. I picked my bag up, pulled out my pass, and walked towards the guard at the entrance.

Rain had fallen on the previous day. No sooner was I inside, where the ground had been trodden by horses and men, than I skated over a rink of mud. But mud was a feature of the camp, as I found out afterwards.

There were no signs of Sunday here; all was as I left it two days before. Hurry and disorder were present; truly there seemed more men, more horses to pull into shape. The same workers passed to and fro; the same loafers chatted amiably in restful corners; the same guards kept weary watch upon their guns.

There was no hurry as far as I was concerned.

From an island in the mud I looked round; and when it was time to move forward, I went no farther than the quartermaster's tent, where the crowd of men and the heaps of stores made progress a matter of tactics. True, my goal was the Brigade Office, and in time I arrived there and stood waiting my turn. It was not long before the clerk beckoned me inside, and for the second time I was before the Colonel. I looked for my acquaintance Sands, who had not put in an appearance. The Colonel spoke a few words; but business soon took his attention, and I stood, baggage in hand, while an orderly went for Captain Knight. Knight was a long time arriving, and finally arrived in a hurry. I found out he commanded the ammunition column. He was quite friendly and talked outside the tent several minutes. He ended by saying, "From now you become Gunner Lake," and then it seemed he recollected a forgotten affair, for he broke off with, "Come on, I'll hand you over to the sergeant-major."

On his heels he turned, and away we went towards the column office, he leading, I following. We passed the cook-house on the way, where a long row of iron pots sat astride the fire. A rickety shed, furnished with a chopping block, basins, and other things, was the only protection from the weather the cooks boasted. A man in a jersey and dungaree trousers peeled potatoes, and a second big fat man chopped up vegetables. That was all there was to see.

The sergeant-major sat in the office, and took

charge of me. I waited a long time while he went through business with a clerk; in truth I was bored to death before he pushed the writing things away and got up. "Come on," he said, and went outside.

In the mud we slipped and slid by men in all dresses and all stages of hurry. The horse-lines were impassable. The stout sergeant-major took matters calmly, trailing me in his wake, with my baggage knocking round my knees. We came in the end to a tent somewhere near the middle of a row and stopped there.

"Corporal Black!" the sergeant-major called out.

A long, nervous-looking man came out of the tent, and stood to attention, staring at us rather stupidly at the same time.

"Corporal," the serjeant-major said, twisting his moustache ends, "this man is going into your tent. His belongings are with him, and you can fix him up with the other things. Start him to-morrow. His name is—what's your name?—Lake."

The corporal introduced himself to me pleasantly enough, and the pair of them fell to talking on other subjects—that is, the sergeant-major talked and the corporal agreed. When the sergeant-major tired and moved away, I was invited into the tent. Black showed me where to sleep, and made me drop my kit there. There were bundles of blankets placed tidily before the tent, and several articles of clothing and equipment hanging from the pole in the centre; but none of the owners were present. The corporal sat on a packing case and I sat down opposite. He looked me all over, twitched his eyelids and began a talk of the camp in general, describing everything as upside down, but telling me I was lucky in my tent, as all the members were good fellows. He did not interest me much, and I passed the time watching events outside. Did I look at him at all, his eyelids started to twitch. Presently he tired of talking, so that a lull fell between us, until he remembered I had not been issued with the regulation blankets and eating utensils. He got up saying we would go to the quartermaster's store, which was close at hand. Out we went. A crowd was about the place; but we got the quartermaster's ear, and quite soon I was loaded up with a waterproof sheet, a pair of blankets, and a knife, fork, spoon, and pannikin.

Back at the tent again, the corporal told me I could do what I liked until twelve o'clock, when the horses went to water. So I started a journey of exploration within the artillery lines, looking at horses, guns, waggons, and everything else. Work had slackened off—men washed at the watertaps, cleaned their leggings, or wrote letters. Behind the ammunition column lines were three batteries. The watering troughs were in a far corner, and the whole camp, appropriately enough, overlooked a cemetery. I was not too exact over the tour, because of the mud, and finding the quartermaster's tent again, I rested on a bagful of harness. Sitting there I saw a sight surely not equalled since Noah organised the march into the ark.

Along the road from the station came men and women and children; not in tens, not in hundreds, but verily in thousands. In cabs they came, in carts, in motors; they came on horses, on bicycles, on their feet. All classes arrived to rub shoulders in the crush. Some walked fast and some walked slowly; some were eager, some lagged behind; some were gay and some depressed. Old and young appeared, mothers, wives, fathers, children, uncles, aunts; in multi-coloured array for an hour they swept by. Baskets, boxes, parcels, handbags came with them, filled, packed, bulging with refreshment for the gallant volunteers. Outside the gate the road grew impassable from vehicles commandeered for the assault; and still foot passengers arrived. It might be an army transport waggon tried to force a passage; but inevitably it jammed in the tide—nor sergeant's threats, nor sergeant's prayers availed it.

The infantry lines swallowed most of the raiders; but enough stayed behind to overflow our grounds. I was sorry to see so many elderly people ploughing through the quagmire; and my sorrow went watching the girls in silk stockings high-stepping through the mud.

Twelve o'clock came, and Corporal Black called out for me to give a hand with the horses. Men in the section were away on leave, which made us short-handed. I have said the water troughs were at the other end of the compound, and in that direction we went. The rule was a man to two horses; and from our column and each of the batteries issued an endless line of horses. At the troughs was a long wait, and then one stood in a couple of inches of water while the horses drank. Back to the lines, we tied up, heel-roped, fed, and were dismissed.

Near our tent I ran into Knight and Sands talking together. Knight looked up, and called me over. "Lake," he said, "the Colonel has made you his galloper, so you will leave the ammunition column and join the Brigade Staff. You are lucky. I would almost as soon have the job as my own. You have more chance of winning a V.C. than any man here." Sands grinned but said nothing. "You'll stay in the column to-day," Knight finished up, "and shift in the morning."

I thanked him and went on. It was good news, and came as a surprise.

At the tent I found it was lunch time. An iron pot of greasy stew was outside, and Corporal Black ladled it out to men standing, plate in hand. The men belonged to the tent, and I was introduced. They seemed good enough fellows.

The stew failed to interest, but it did not matter, for we were given no time to eat it. An order came along that horses had arrived for us, and we must fall in at once. Everyone started to grumble, but out we had to go. About a hundred men formed up in two ranks, and when there had been sundry conferences of officers and a running about of N.C.O.'s, we marched out of the gates at a smart pace. The crowd still arrived from the station, though not in great numbers; and the road was absolutely blocked with waiting vehicles. It was impossible to keep rank, and the order was given to fall out. The horses were in a yard by the road, drafted into pairs by remount men, and each one of us led a pair back to camp.

The afternoon wore on, and by the time the horses were picketed the trumpeter had blown "Water" and "Feed." This brought the day's work to an end. I had tea—bread and jam and tea—and wandered forth on a second journey of discovery. I watched the crowd of soldiers and visitors talking and making love, until closing hour arrived and the latter disappeared.

Finally the camp was empty of strangers. The stars came out, evening aged into night, and the big enclosure was hushed. There was impatient stamping of horses, there were the voices of pickets passing down the lines: nothing more. I found the way back to my tent.

In the ground I hollowed a hip-hole, spread out the waterproof sheet, and over it laid the blankets. The clothes I took off afterwards made the pillow. I lay down and covered myself up. The others drifted in and made their own beds.

Listening to the murmur of voices, watching shadows thrown from the one candle by the tent-pole, I heard blown the "First Post," the "Last Post," and "Lights Out."

The week which followed brought endless bitter winds and uncharitable showers. Not one sunny smile had it for the recruit.

At break of day "Réveillé" sounded through

the camp. With the last notes, I threw the blankets off, rubbed my eyes and with an effort got up. The tent was open, showing a leaden sky where late stars hurried away. The horses in the lines stood with drooping heads; and a picket, muffled to the eyes, wandered along at funeral pace.

In the tent no one moved: breathing was even and serene. However, I started to dress; and presently Corporal Black rolled over, sighed and poked a nose out of the blankets. "Was that 'Réveillé'?" he said huskily. I nodded. He lay quite still, blinking his eyes; but growing more awake, presently he sat up, and from his seat surveyed the slumberers. Then he woke up in a hurry. "Get up there, you fellows," he began to shout. "'Réveillé's' gone ten minutes!" Right and left he leaned, shaking all he could reach; and slowly, and with many groans and an oath or two, the tent awoke. By now I was dressed, and I left him doing his worst.

A second call sounded almost at once, and ten minutes later the "Fall in" went. From every tent men came tumbling, some without leggings, some drawing on their coats, half of the company with boots unlaced. A few arrived from the watertaps with shining faces; and all headed towards the parade ground beside the quartermaster's tent. In lines, one behind another, we fell in; and, with the last stragglers still doubling up, the roll was called. In five minutes the brigade marched into stables.

The routine was yesterday's—watering, grooming, and feeding. When we turned out, breakfast was ready. Breakfast meant a small chop, bread and jam. After breakfast we paraded again for stables and exercising. Exercising over, there was watering and feeding to go through. Then along came lunch—stew and bread and jam.

I was sitting outside the tent, persuading myself we had finished a damned good dinner, when I found a little corporal standing close by. He was short, fat, and very young. When I looked up, he came forward and began to speak in a hesitating fashion.

"You are Lake, aren't you?" he said.

"Yes," I answered, getting up.

"My name is Tank. I am corporal of the Brigade Staff. You've been put on to the Staff, you know, and I've come along to tell you to bring any baggage to our tent. We're the four tents at the end of the row; but if you'll come along now, I can give you a hand."

I thanked him and put things together. I told Corporal Black what was happening, and soon was ready to start. The fellows in the tent nodded goodbye and then we left. The new corporal was quite good-natured, insisting on carrying some of the things.

A number of men sat by the Brigade Staff tents, contemplating without interest the remains of the late feast. They looked me over with casual stares; but the corporal said nothing. He led the way into the second tent, which was empty except for blankets in their waterproof covers. "Take the empty place over there," he said, pointing with his hand. I dropped my blankets and other gear where he suggested, and while I did this he pulled a lot of chocolate from his pocket, handing me a large piece and filling his own mouth. "You'll be all right," he said. "I have to go up to Brigade Office now. Don't go away, as we fall in soon." He hesitated a moment, and then went through the doorway.

I arranged my kit in a better way, for there was no room to spare, and then followed him out. The other fellows of the Staff still sat and lay round the tents; but I knew none of them, and walked a little way off towards the parade ground.

There had been a few gleams of sun about midday; but it was getting bitterly cold again. Half the men had on their coats, and the horses in the lines were rugged up. I pushed my hands into my pockets and turned my back to the wind. I was not exactly hungry, but the stew could have been more interesting.

"Aye, my friend, behind you the gates are closed. Uncharitable skies and stony beds henceforth shall be your portion. Months shall it be ere you taste of comfort's draught again. Though your tears be bitter, none but yourself shall mourn, for yours—yours was the choice."

The trumpeter blew "Fall in," and I doubled for the parade ground; fast behind me the others hurried up. After roll call Corporal Tank marched the Staff to the back of the Brigade Office tent, and formed us up in two rows. Then he disappeared inside. He had been gone a very little time before the bitter winds tested and found wanting our slender discipline. The men began to shuffle their feet, to twist about, and next to break rank. A pair started a boxing match, others played leap-frog. What remained turned spectators or broke out into cursing the weather and themselves as fools for volunteering. Before long not a man was in his place; and behold, without warning, from the tent stepped forth dramatically my old acquaintance Sands himself. He gave a preliminary stony stare, before bursting into wrath.

"What in God's name do you think you're doing? Is this a parade or a damned circus? I don't know how a lot of bally fools like you managed to join; you must have escaped from the nursery! Fall in at once! Next time all leave is stopped!"

He had by no means finished. He tried indignation and failed; he tried sarcasm and failed; he tried appealing to our feelings and failed utterly. In the end he was incoherent and collapsed.

The corporal had followed him from the tent with a bundle of flags, white and blue. These were handed round.

"Now we're doing station work this afternoon," Sands announced with a blow of his nose. "Have you all got pencils and paper?" Nobody had anything. "Oh, how absolutely damnable!" He beat the air. "What do you mean by coming out like this? You are worse than babies! Go and get them. The next man that comes out without a pencil can consider himself under arrest!" From the abashed ranks an individual wandered forth in search of pencils. Sands watched with darkening brow. "Double, man, double!" he screamed at last. The figure broke into a heavy canter and was lost among the tents.

While we waited, Sands and the corporal held a conference. It was not possible to hear what was said; but at the end of it Sands turned about with the order, "Fall out those men who have done no semaphore signalling." Half a dozen of us stepped forward, I among them. "Take these men, Corporal, start them on the alphabet. They won't want flags. See that you keep them at it: there is very little time for this sort of thing." The corporal saluted, Sands saluted. The corporal cried, "'Shun! Right turn, quick march," and away we went over the mud to a deserted corner. "Halt! Left turn. Stand at ease": and there we were in line facing him.

The afternoon was full of hurrying clouds—restless, cheerless clouds—and the eager winds which had roamed all day over the open country swooped gladly upon me. I found a handkerchief and blew my nose lustily, cursing at heart the corporal for choosing such a barren spot. He on his own account looked blue and uneasy; but his fat helped him.

"Pay attention," he said. The squad looked up. In short jerky sentences he explained the principles of signalling, illustrating the position of "Prepare to signal," and other matters. Presently we stood at "Prepare." "Now we'll try the first circle—Ak to G. To prevent mistakes,

A is pronounced Ak, B is Beer, D is Don. Now commence. Ak, Beer, C, Don; E, F, G.

Away went his arm, and away after it went ours. "Again now. Repeat. Repeat again." Round and round the circle went our arms, with many halts and delays. It was tiring and bitterly cold work; but we were kept at it. All the while I could hear the beating of boughs in the pine trees behind, and could see tents pulling at their guys and rugs flapping on the horses.

Sands had formed up in pairs the remainder of the Staff, one pair opposite another pair, and these pairs waved flags and did sundry other things. For the first half-hour a fair amount of work was got through; but it happened that Sands had an appointment, or grew tired or cold or something, for he disappeared and left the signalling to its fate. A tall fellow called Oxbridge threw down his flags at once. "Damn this," he said, and fell on to the ground. The others followed him; and though Tank walked across and threatened, nobody cared. So he came back to us again; and set us at our Ak, Beer, C. One by one the other party drew together, and soon a pleasant little conversation went forward, spoilt only by the inclement afternoon.

At last Tank dismissed us for a few minutes' spell. The fellows wandered off in different directions, while Tank came over to me and attempted a conversation. He struck me as a curious chap, dissatisfied with things, yet unready to make efforts to right them. I began to suspect him as a poor disciplinarian; he on the contrary blamed the muddled condition of affairs to Sands, who, he said, was no good and heart-breaking to work under. I listened but poorly, it was too cold, and, turning on his heels presently, he ordered the signallers to fall in anew, which they did after argument. Round and round went our arms again until the trumpeter blew "Stables."

All that week wind and storm prevailed, and all the week we stood in the open signalling. At the end of three or four days there was no man who was not sneezing, sniffling, and coughing.

Week by week it was the same thing. It was stables, stables, stables; and signalling, signalling, signalling, with now and then a lesson on the director, plotter, or rangetaker, and now and then a lecture. The lectures were before a blackboard in a tent; Sands gave them, and halfway through he would become tangled up beyond vaguest hope of extrication. But that was small matter to him. He would go outside and read up what he had forgotten, and come back and bounce us. We had riding drill, and we practised galloping in and out of action; also we had small manœuvres on our own account, and, things shaping better, the complete brigade manœuvred presently, first alone, afterwards in combination with the infantry.

The camp endured several weeks, and during that time the weather did not change. Very soon every man was sick to death of the whole affair. It was belief in our quick departure that alone sustained us. For constantly it was rumoured we were about to start on our great adventure, and once or twice we went as far as to make preparation. Disappointment was not borne in silence. But most things come at last. One dark and chilly morning found us clattering through Melbourne streets on the road to the wharf.

CHAPTER IV

THE VOYAGE

OUR boat, the *Blankshire,* put out of Albany Harbour one of a fleet of transports fifty or more strong, convoyed by cruisers. We began a weary journey to an unknown destination, fair winds and fair skies companioning us. The fleet steamed in three lines, travelling at the fastest rate of the slowest vessel, and the convoy moved abeam, to starboard and to port.

The *Blankshire* had steamed through Port Phillip Bay a fortnight before, carrying a sober ship's company. We had left camp at the eleventh hour, and few friends were on the wharf to call goodbye. To help us, it may be, the band played on the boat deck through early afternoon, until the trumpeter blew "Stables."

At last land had been exchanged for sea; but it was out of the frying-pan into the fire. We moved into the swelter of the tropics, and routine gripped us. It was stables, stables, stables! It was stables before breakfast, and stables after breakfast; stables in the afternoon, and stable picket at night. Across the jumble of trampled men and nervous horses came for ever Sands's voice.

"You fellows, keep those horses moving. What are you doing there, Oxbridge? Why aren't you hand-rubbing, Woods?"

Round and round the steaming decks moved the procession of men and horses, a battered, unsavoury collection, long lost to hope. Through the middle of the day, when the sun was most menacing, we spelled for a couple of hours, lying about the decks to doze and read. After tea we loitered in the same way, and those who could brave the stifling lower decks went below to gamble. On pay nights you would find a gambling school at half the mess tables, with gold and notes passing forward and backward. Many a man left the table lighter in pocket, if heavier at heart. Towards ten o'clock "Lights out" was blown, the hammocks would be slung on their hooks, and we would turn in for the night, packed like sardines. You could not move an elbow. And so another day ended.

But who wants the details of that weary journey? Heat and the odour of manure are what best I remember of it. It seemed never more would we sight land.

One afternoon there came an order we must show no lights after dark, and night falling, the fleet moved forward in gloom. And one fine day the *Sydney* steamed into the horizon, and at morning stables arrived the news she had met and sunk the *Emden*. A great cheer went up, one of the few cheers passing our lips for many a day. But we saw nothing of the fight ourselves, and the weeks went by full of a long monotony. But it was ordained we should have a foretaste of the great adventure ahead of us. It happened thus.

A red-hot sun went down into the ocean, and a calm, close night had fallen. The troopdecks, with hundreds of hammocks rocking gently against one another, were stifling. The sounds of hundreds of sleepers came out of the dark, for rays of the sentry's lantern at the companion-top crept no farther than the stairway bottom. Through the port-holes the stars moved up and down, and through the port-holes came the shifting of the seas.

They had inoculated me a second time that day, and I lay in a hammock between decks, burnt with a slow fever. I turned and turned; but I could not sleep. There was not a breath of air. I saw the old sentry relieved, and the new man take his seat beside the lantern to read and nod. The dark was full of the little noises of sleepers—rustlings, strange breathings, short-lived groans, jumbled snatches of talk. Sometimes these noises died while I dozed, next I would grow wide awake. Heartily I wished the night gone.

I forget what I thought about—nothing, it may be. I remember waking and dozing, dozing and waking, that is all. Finally the night wore on towards morning, and the fever began to wear out of me. It seemed at last I was wooing sleep.

With a great roar of waters, an unbelievable shock, and a grinding of timbers, the *Uranus* struck us astern, came on, and struck us again amidships. With a roar of waters, she fell back into the dark. An instant of silence came, and hard on it followed the frantic hooting of the siren, and the sentry came falling down the companion, the lantern tumbling atop of him. We were left in the dark.

The shock of collision had set every hammock wildly swinging and had left me wide awake. In one movement my legs were over the side of the hammock, and I had pulled down the lifebelt from the rack above. All over the troop-deck you heard men waking up in a hurry, clinging to the hammocks on either side to steady themselves, pulling themselves into upright positions, and reaching out for lifebelts. There was a sense of great fear in us. For as long as it takes to tell no one spoke, next voices piped out all over the place.

"Collision, boys, collision!" someone called out. And someone else cried, "It's a dinkum collision this time!" And a score of other voices were exclaiming. It was very dark, so much so that almost nothing could be discovered; but there were the sounds of men reaching about or jumping on to the tables, and the quick patter of many naked feet on the floor. In no time men streamed up the companion, fastening lifebelts as they went or carrying them under their arms.

I had wasted no time in jumping on to the

ground; but I paused a minute to pull on my boots and get an overcoat, for I liked little the idea of a voyage in an open boat in pyjamas. I paused no more than a moment, but at the bottom of the companion I found myself on the outside edge of an excited crowd surging in a single direction.

The night was very calm, and as soon as the ship had ceased to quiver she became quite steady. Her engines had stopped; but as yet there was no list or anything of that kind. It was the darkness and the sense of being trapped below that made one hold one's breath. Men who had slept on deck were trying to get down for their belts, and we in much larger numbers were pushing up. There was a jam in the tide. You heard men calling out, "Keep to the right, keep to the right!" or "Steady on there with your blasted pushing!" Then I was caught in the flood and carried quite slowly up the companion, and vomited forth on to the open deck.

Now either it had rained, or the dews were very heavy, or the crew had been in act of hosing down the deck; but the first thing I found coming out into the open was that the deck ran water. "By Jove, she's going quickly," thought I! The place was crowded with men moving fast in all directions; but I turned sharp to the right and got a footing on the second companion, leading to the upper deck. The same crowd pushed up and down here; but I was caught again and emptied out on top as had happened before. I had been behindhand down below, and up here I found many of the men formed up before their boat stations, lifebelts on, and the officer in command calling the roll. I hurried past to our own collision station, and found most of the Staff there, and Sands in charge, quite cool and on the bounce as best became him.

He eyed me coldly as I fell into line. "Lake, you are too slow to catch your shadow! Silence there in the ranks! You fellows ought to know by this time there is to be absolute silence. The next man who speaks will go under arrest."

It was a beautiful night. The sky was full of stars, there was no wind, and the air was very warm. We had come to a standstill, and the water about us was sleepy and full of shadows, and alive with quick sparkles of phosphorus when you looked down into it. All about were the lights of the other transports, which seemed to have stopped; and I found myself peering into the dark to find if the lifeboats were arriving.

The hurry of the first moments was over now, the men were lined up before their boat stations, and the only movements were of the boats' crews unlashing the tarpaulin coverings and arranging the tackle and the oars. I was wondering at the strangeness of the calm after all the hubbub, when from near the funnel a rocket went up into the air with a great rush. It hung a long moment high up in the sky, while the lot of us craned necks after it. The calm night, and the quiet which had fallen over the ship, had loosened the grip of fear on most of us, until this sudden signal rushed into the heavens. Now men began to look sideways at one another, and you might see men licking their lips. The only light about here came up from the engine-room, by way of an open hatch, and those standing near-by peered down, for what reason I could not guess. The Morse lights began to wink from neighbouring transports; but other answer to our signal than this I could not find. A second rocket hissed into the air.

I looked for a list to starboard or to port; but none did I make out. The lifeboat in front of us rocked ever so gently in the davits; and this might mean a list or only the heaving of the seas. I could not decide, and I looked again for the lifeboats which the other transports should have sent.

Truly it was eerie work standing silent in the dark, knowing nothing and guessing overmuch. There was no noise beyond the clatter of movement made by the seamen unlacing the tarpaulin of our lifeboat, shifting the oars, and examining the lockers. Half a dozen were at the work and seemed to take the affair calmly enough, all but one who fussed about in an agitated manner until told to go and bury himself. And Sands—the unquenchable Sands—marched solemnly up and down before us, the lifebelt drawn high under his armpits and lending him in the gloom a hunchback appearance.

For an hour and more we stood there.

After what seemed a night of waiting, two men went round the lower deck with a lantern, peering here and there as though making search. In course of time they stopped by a lifeboat on the port side, and one cried out in a great rough voice: "Prepare to lower boat!" I had watched him as he shouted, and now there came a shine in the waters beyond the rail, and I discovered floatly calmly, and it seemed most tragically, an overturned boat. It bobbed up and down twice or thrice, then moved into the gloom, and I lost it. The man with the lantern and a number of other fellows grouped round the lifeboat in the davits; but whether they lowered it or not I did not discover. It was impossible to follow their movements where I was.

We stayed on at our stations, whispering and shifting from one leg to another; and nothing happening beyond the turning of the stars, and the listing of the seas, a sense of security returned. Finally a hint of dawn crept into the sky.

Now as we stood, full weary of waiting and impatient of the slow dawn, a shaft of yellow light fell on us from afar, picking us out of the dark, and setting a-shining the seas about us, and behold, H.M.S. *Hernshaw* was drawing alongside. She moved within hailing distance, under her own way it seemed, the glare of her lights falling over her guns and her armoured sides. Her decks were cleared for action. Aft of her were paraded her crew; an officer, megaphone in hand, in command. She moved within hailing distance of us, a creature of brilliant lights and gloomy shadows; a creature at once so beautiful and so forbidding that I forgot my last fears watching her.

The officer put the megaphone to his mouth. "Are you all right?" There came an answer from our bridge, which I lost. But the man-of-war's reply was plain to hear. "Then what are you waiting for?" Again I lost our answer. Hard on it followed the man-of-war's command. "Pick up your boat at once and go on!"

Their searchlights had travelled up and down our starboard side; now they shut off, and the *Hernshaw* moved into the dark. Quite soon she had slipped away; next our engines beat again, and the screws began to turn. We were moving on. There came the order, "Dismiss!" A half light had crept everywhere, and you saw men pour down the companions to the lower decks in pyjamas and shirts, talking and pulling off lifebelts on the way. On the lower deck I ran into Sands, who had come down by another companion. Our eyes met, and he gave me a great understanding grin.

Delays went for nothing, and presently we drew near the coast of Egypt. We held a concert on the boatdeck to celebrate our coming, the stars shining above us, and the blue phosphorus-filled water swirling below. To wind up, Colonel Irons told us he had news to give. Egypt, not England, was our destination. There was work to be done, and we might be fighting in a few days.

The jaded company took heart again. Soon we lay off Port Saïd among a fleet of warboats and other craft; and later we lay against a wharf at Alexandria, and the long voyage was at an end.

CHAPTER V

IN EGYPT

EAVES put his hairy hands upon my shoulder, and dragged me out of sleep. " 'Ere, Lake, wake up, you're on picket with me!" I opened my eyes and looked at him. "My God," said I. Eaves grinned and moved away. He wore his overcoat, and a helmet of wool over head and neck. The big black moustache hid the rest of his face. "Show a leg this way!" he called back, plunging hands into pockets and hunching his shoulders. Away he went.

I lay nearly atop of Tank, one blanket serving both of us. I got up quietly to leave him undisturbed, and tucked him up at the same time. He was on his side, an arm across his face; and he was full of deep breaths. We had lain down as we had arrived a couple of hours before. I got up fully dressed. The sand had grown cold and had gathered much dew, and I was rheumy and knew a hundred little pains. I threw one arm above my head, and after it the other. I tossed back my head and opened my mouth, letting go something between a yawn and an oath.

It was night yet; but dawn was very near. The sand was hidden under a grey vapour; the sky was cloudless and filled with stars. To the right hand there seemed uneven hills climbing into the sky; and to the left, in the distance, stood the Pyramids. In the centre of this desert space was the little company of men and horses, sleeping exhaustion's sleep. We had staggered there, and straightway had thrown ourselves upon the sand.

I stepped clear of everybody until I was in the open. I stamped my feet, settled my coat, pulled straight the wool helmet. I was dead tired still. Then I turned the way Eaves had gone, leaving behind me the sleepers. The horses were tethered to a single headline and lacked heelropes. Some lay on their sides without twitch of the ear or quiver of the nostril; others were stretched out, breathing in great sighs. There were those that got up, shifted a pace or two, and dropped down again; and those that wandered until pulled up by the rope or entangled with a neighbour, when they reared or plunged in spiritless manner. Never had I looked on such a weary company.

Hands in pockets, Eaves wandered up and down, grumbling to himself and shouting at the horses. Quickly it was seen the absent heelropes caused work in plenty. We dived together for a brute on his knees, half choked with a tangled headline; and we dived again for another in worse case. Hardly was there time to swear at each other: there was no time for yawning. Of course there were lulls in the fury when we stood a few moments straight-backed to stare at the ground or look one another in the eyes, and curse Egypt and the Kaiser and ourselves as fools for having come this far. And then it was "Blast that 'orse!" and together we sprang for it. The wide flat country shut in by blue starry sky made the night immense, and we went about much of our work in silence. For the small noises of our movements and our words, and the groans of the horses, were caught and swallowed instantly in the stillness. There was so much to do, time went with great speed. The false dawn moved abroad while I thought still it was night.

We were on short picket, and quite soon I was relieved. Light was spreading everywhere, the fog was lifting, and with it passed away the damp. The morning was very sharp, so that I started to wonder how long the sun would delay. As yet there was no sign of it. I waited a few moments, hands deep in pockets, watching the new pickets move disconsolately up and down. Then I walked back to the sleepers. They were as I had left them, on their backs with open mouths, curled up knees to chin, and even covered completely up in coat or blanket. Even now it wanted most of an hour to réveillé, and I thought of bed again. Tank had seized the blanket for himself; but I knelt down and firmly took most of it away. He groaned, but he did not wake up. I lay down beside him and pushed my back against his, which was warm and comforting after the sharp air. I wrapped the blanket well about me, and quite soon I was asleep.

I seemed asleep no time at all; but when I woke the sun had come up into the sky, the desert was bright and alive, and men were waking all round me, yawning, getting up, and stamping, and cursing Egypt for a barren and barbarous land. Tank sat beside me, blinking his eyes, and puffing his cheeks out like a swollen toad. He was dirty and done up, and I knew his liver was out of order again. It meant a bad time for the Staff, had not the Staff taken Tank's wrath as a joke. I forget if we spoke at the time. I know presently I rose to my feet and walked a little way off from the others. I felt as broken up as I could wish to be, stiff and dirty and not overfull of hope. It was the sharpness of the morning that saved me. I took off the woollen helmet and opened out my coat, and in a few minutes my blood began to move a little. I thought of a wash; but, hands deep in pockets and legs apart, first I saw what was to be seen.

We were a ragged island of men and horses dropped in a sea of sand. Around was a vast stretch of country, hill land and flat land covered deeply with fine sand. Where I stood the floor was printed over with marks of men and beasts; but farther away the sand sparkled virgin and unsoiled, as though for ages no life had passed by. It was a sombre and forbidding land, and yet it attracted me strangely. In front, a mile or so away, the country was relieved by an oasis of palms many hundred acres in extent. A considerable village of mud huts had grown up on the outskirts, and now in and out the gates wandered what looked like flocks of goats and sheep, tended by native children. There seemed a building or two solitary among the palms, and tall robed figures moved among the trees and round about the village. A man led to work a string of three camels, and other men sat astride ambling donkeys, their legs sweeping the ground. And there were curious cattle shambling before a leisurely cowherd. The shrill crying of voices and the barking of dogs came constantly from over there. Farther to the right ran the straight road to Cairo. It was marked for several miles of its length by two lines of trees. We had brought the horses that way last night, or this morning, to tell the truth. The desert seemed to march beyond the farther side; but it was not easy to see past the trees.

Swinging farther still to the right hand, I met the Pyramids. Where I stood two only were visible. They rose up side by side, large and very forbidding. Before them had risen the first tents of the camp. There seemed, also, stacks of stores in building. Troops moved about in the neighbourhood, like ourselves the vanguard of the great camp. Behind me the desert stretched bare of everything to the horizon. So much for the present, thought I, and I went back to the others.

All the men were awake now, and, as we had lain down in our clothes, there was little toilet to perform. All seemed short of temper, for they were blinking at one another and cursing their luck. That merry rogue Wilkes alone of them all greeted me with smiling face. He sat cross-kneed on a waterproof sheet, and called out to know how I did. I stopped by him and looked down. He was an Englishman, a jolly vagabond chap, and a liar of wonderful ability. I had a strange liking for him; he was my best tonic for the blues. I had but to call out: "Wilkes, old man, come and lie to me about your rich uncle," and across he would come and keep me smiling for an hour.

Now he turned to me his white, well-fed face, which made me think of a shifty parson, and cried out: "What d'you make of it, Lake?"

I shrugged my shoulders, and said nothing.

"The same here," he answered, laughing.

Oxbridge, who had been growling to himself, chipped in from near-by. "Awful place! Wish I was back in Collins Street. Won't catch me here again."

Then Tank came at us on the bounce and shut us up. He jerked out his sentences on the end of his breath. "What are you doing there! Get up at once! Fall in! D'you want to be told a hundred times! Oxbridge, what are you doing there! D'you hear me, Oxbridge!"

"I damned well hear you," said Oxbridge, rising leisurely to his feet.

The sun rose up, a kindly sun, warm but not too hot; and the earth grew more cheerful. The winds sparkled and the distant palm leaves glittered; but the bite in the air stayed. The horses were little recovered by their rest, and still lay as dead, with bodies turned gratefully towards the sun. The pickets wandered forwards and backwards along the line. We had expected a day's rest; but we started the weariest day in my memory. There was chaff to be humped over the sand for the horses; there was watering to be done. The shifting sands made walking a labour in itself. Later we were given the camping ground allotted us; it was distant from the old spot, and quantities of baggage must be carried there. The journeys over the sand were endless.

There was baggage which proved too weighty for man-handling, and a party of us were told off to commandeer help. We trudged towards the tented area, and found there a great gathering of rickety lorries, drawn in each case by a thin underbred horse, and driven by an unsavoury native. The vehicles were in much confusion, there was constant backing, grinding, and jarring; and the drivers employed frenzied gestures and wild shouts. Outside this gathering were a score of resting camels, thrusting this way and that snaky heads, or rolling jaws from side to side on the cud. A group of drivers squatted on their hams, pulling to pieces in their fingers round flat cakes, and pushing the fragments into their mouths. Like the horses, the camels were stale and unkempt; and the gorgeously robed drivers would have been the better for a wash.

We stood a short while watching the jumble, perhaps as we were uncertain of the method of possessing these transports. The soldiers quartered down here were English Territorials, belonging to a Manchester Regiment. I was told they had been sent over from Cairo to prepare camp for us. It was to be seen they knew the game better than ourselves, as he who wanted a cart or camel plunged into the tide, chose a beast more promising than the rest, jumped upon the driver, and by threats and promises forced him to thread a way into the open. The confusion increased, the voices of the drivers broke into passionate Arabic; there was a cracking of whips and a grinding of wheels; and finally lorry or camel came into the quiet of the more open ways and moved over the desert.

The quartermaster's tents were rigged here, and men weighed out meat, flour, and vegetables, and loaded them on the lorries. The crush in the lanes between the tents was great, lorries, camels, and soldiers trying to pass at the same time. Oaths in plenty were to be heard for the listening, but a current of good nature ran under all. It did not take us long to learn our part. We secured our lorries, heedless of groans and protests from the drivers that they had worked all night and could do no more. We crowded on to them, dangling our legs over the back, and turned towards last night's camping ground. The sand made the going very heavy, and the horses were underbred and starved. We were sorry for them, but we were sorrier for ourselves and stayed where we were. Torrents of Arabic and a heavy whip got us home at last.

As yet the camp had neither boundaries nor guards, and natives overran it. Numbers came to loaf and stare; also there were orange sellers in scores, and vendors of nougat, chocolate, picture postcards, and cigarettes. They grew a nuisance with their importunity. This was our first day, and we accepted them in good humour and bought largely. The news of our wealth spread quickly, and turned the camp into a travelling bazaar, with merchants ready to bargain salvation at a price.

It was coming towards the middle of the morning, the sun was high up, the sharpness in the air gone, yet the heat was in no way oppressive. The winter climate was ideal. I own the prospect of endless sand was very desolate, and the men seemed to think so. To tell the truth, we were dog-tired, and the endless marching across the sands was taking the last of our spirit from us. Matters were little improved now the lorries helped us. With quite a moderate load aboard, the wheels sank into the sand; and pull the weedy beast as he might, and scream the driver as he could, the load waited where it was. So it happened we must push and haul at the wheel-spokes, or put a shoulder behind the waggon; and in this way, with imprecations and many rests, the baggage shifted ground. We wore out the morning on these journeys.

A dozen natives under a white overseer sank holes for our horse-lines. Never have I met a more easy-going company. Three shovelfuls per minute was the average. The digger put his shovel into the ground and leaned a foot on it; and looked long at the sky and longer at us, and next pressed home the shovel. He straightened his back then, said a word to a neighbour, and lifted out the sand. There was something noble in the leisure of those movements. I watched the gang as I lay on the sand eating a makeshift lunch.

The transport of material continued through the afternoon and into the evening; nor did our sorrows end until fresh chaff had been brought over and the horses watered and fed. To be honest, we managed a few spells for ourselves during that time. There was a great deal to see. People passed constantly to and from the village on camels and donkeys; and herds tended cattle, sheep, and goats not far away. There was no false modesty: we stared at them; they stared at us. There were the bright-robed fruit-sellers, money-changers, guides, cigarette merchants, vendors of silks, chocolates, picture postcards with whom to argue. All this took time. There had been no space to rig tents, and we lay down again at night on the open sands. The desert was not a bad bedroom, the sky being cloudless and full of bright stars. But the sun had not long gone down before the night grew very cold and made a mock of blankets and overcoats. I turned once or twice before morning.

CHAPTER VI

THE SOLDIER'S LIFE

THE camp grew apace. A great area, reaching nearly to the shadow of the Pyramids, became covered over with tents; and many thousand men and horses arrived down the long road from Cairo. The infantry quartered themselves at the upper end, where the floor of the desert narrowed to a valley climbing into the hills; light horse took the desert's inner edge; and army service and we artillery formed the triangle's base, nearest the palm grove. Steamrollers and gangs of native workmen drove roads across the sands, reservoirs were built, wash troughs for the men were put up and watering troughs for the horses. The camp continued to grow and to improve.

Our first week was an evil one. We could not find our true position, so that several times the horse-lines were relaid. Our tents were pitched and repitched. And the sand, meeting us as strangers, was wearying beyond belief. We set to wondering hard whether a soldier's life would suit us. But the start was the worst: there followed a change for the better.

Réveillé tumbled us out of bed on many a

frosty morning. I say "tumbled us out of bed," but I mean turned us on our pillows, for it was Tank's jerky voice which would not be denied. About thirty of us slept in a large tent, where the first morning lights came in through the open doorways to lift the gloom and discover the forms of the sleepers. We were packed tight, with arms thrown over one another and mouths open. Some men would be gone altogether under a heap of clothing. Most mornings I sat up with the last notes of the trumpet, for I was slow at dressing. It might be someone else would rise to rub eyes and swear, but not often; the sleepers rolled over, though maybe a fellow blinked and covered himself up again or lit a cigarette. And then Tank's jerky sentences broke the peace. "Get up! Get up at once! What are you doing there! Didn't you hear Réveillé? Get up there!" Still slumbered on the tent. The voice started again. "Get up! Get up, I say. Réveillé's gone! I'll peg any man who doesn't get up!" There might now follow a movement among the sleepers, and with many a groan the tent would awake.

It was wise to make an early start dressing. Between "Réveillé" and "Fall in" the interval was not long, and blankets must be rolled for inspection and kits stacked outside by them. As all the fellows waited for the last few minutes and dressed together, there was great scramble and confusion. When the "Fall in" went, men still were running about, dumping down their kits, putting on leggings, and pulling on coats.

We fell in in two rows at the end of our lines, and Tank called the roll.

Sands's habit was to stroll across in the middle, and stand huddled in a greatcoat, for he resisted the cold but indifferently. His face showed very pinched and trembling, and he had much use for a handkerchief. The roll call over, he read brigade orders, and maybe he added a few remarks of his own upon our habits. Then came the first command of the day. "Turn in! Cast off for water!" The rule was a man to two horses, but more often it was a man to three or four. Those who stayed behind cleaned up the lines and filled the nosebags, and a man went down to the camels to bring up the day's fodder. The journey to the water was tedious and not without risk; but the vast congregation of horses at the other end was a wonderful sight. There were many thousand moving to and fro. Halfway on the road there, we met the sun rising behind the trees on the Cairo highway. It was of immense size and blood red, and the long rays swept across the desert, and set the horses' backs shining. At once the chill left the sands, though the cold stayed.

Often there was a long wait in the neighbourhood of the troughs, as the water supply was wont to give out. Such times were spent calling to the other fellows, begging cigarettes, or watching the happenings at the village not far away. The place was for ever full of peasants moving about their work. Women went down to the waterhole, bearing on their heads large earthenware pots;

children tended the flocks and herds; and the men worked at their cultivation and led away into the palms camels and bullocks. There was always a shrill crying of voices from over there, and a barking of mongrel dogs. In time our turn came; we moved on to the troughs; the horses saw the water and made a plunge for it, and there was a breathless moment while they steadied down. They were given plenty of time to drink. Presently sounded Sands's voice: "Staff, files left! Walk, march!" and we joined the great procession moving back to the lines.

On the return we heelroped and began the morning grooming. I rode a big bony horse, who had known better days as a steeplechaser. He was so full of angles I named him "The Director"; but he was an honest hack. It was my daily penance to tend his wants and polish his coat, and slender enough results did my labours bring me. All the sands of the desert made a target of him; and many a measure of special feed went down his throat without filling his hide. Yet I forgave him much, for he was a good friend.

The men working on the feed passed down the rear of the lines, planting a bag behind each horse. Sands walked up and down the horses' heads, watching the grooms from the tail of his eye. Here and there he stopped and made examination. Often he suspected me. Frequently he came up and rubbed his hand through "The Director's" coat. On unlucky days a shower of sand flew out. "Lake," he screamed once, "the condition of this horse is worthy of a court-martial.

I thought you knew something about horses! I see you never saw a horse before you came here! That's not the way to use a brush, man! Give it to me!" He seized the brush and rubbed with great vigour until the dust went into his eyes and nose. Then he fled for another victim. Sands maddened most of his men; but he only amused me. There was something likeable deep down in him. I am sure he saw the humour of his doings. Often I caught him smiling as he turned away.

When we were all full weary in the arm, and the professional loafers had disappeared on one errand or another, Sands would bethink him of breakfast. "In rear of your horses!" came the order. "Stand to your nosebags! Pick up your dressing on the right there! Oxbridge, do you hear me!" On these occasions Tank stationed himself at one end of the line and wagged his hand in an agitated way. "Pick up your dressing there; pick up your dressing!" he cried in jerky notes. Then Sands called out again. "Are you ready to feed, Corporal?" "Yes, sir." "Feed, trumpeter!" And the trumpeter blew "Feed."

Of all the good comrades who had come on this expedition—of those, I mean, who could drive the devil of tedium from you at least notice—there was none better than the trumpeter. He could tell a wittier story than anyone else; he could tell a story more wittily than anyone else; he could act better, mimic better, dance better, lie better, laugh better than anyone in the tent; he could do anything that helped to hurry time. Night after night he was the centre of a shaking circle. If half his tales were true he had lived a strange life. He was full of energy and full of resource, and carried a stout heart in his body. To a dispirited army he was worth a battery of guns. There were other fellows on the staff. There were public-school men like Hawkins and Jimmy Bull; there was Woods who never looked dirty, and Stokes who never looked clean. There was big Bill Eaves who always was crying out, and yet was a good man. There was Mossback from the bush who had brains in place of education; and Corporal Baker who took life heavily and was a good man at his work, though he would have been the better for a wash. There was Wilkinson, tall, lean, and dark; and Lewis, tall and fair, with the face of a girl. There were others to tell you of some day.

"Cookhouse" was blown soon after the "Turn out." In these early days we squatted on our kitbags, plates on knees, and chewed up sand with the bread and meat. Later we were given tables and forms, and mess-houses were built us. But at first, as I say, we sat down in the sand to eat, and the food was rough and not plentiful.

A canteen was opened near our lines, where you could buy a few things at a heavy price to help down the bread and sand. We spent a good deal of our money there, so that most breakfast times saw us emptying sardines and salmon on to our plates. And it was "Pass the blasted bread there!" and, "Fer Gawd's sike, pass the jam!"

The first weeks of our arrival brigade orders forbade the riding of a single horse, and we exercised them about the desert in long files at the cost of our legs. Tramping in the sand was heartbreaking work, and we marched miles a day; but the mornings were exhilarating, and the day never grew too warm. There was no threat of the evil summer to follow. Our journey led us among the sandhills, where we were lost to sight of everything but dismal sweeps of sand. Or we topped a rise and were shown afar off the palm groves on the desert edge, and beyond them the great city of Cairo. To the right hand stood the Pyramids, and past them a vast stretch of desert dotted with solitary palms, and palms in groves, and near the skyline other Pyramids. It was splendid to halt up here and overlook the wide country. The orange sellers, trailing gorgeous rags, followed us, and you might lie a few minutes sucking cool oranges, forgetful of the drudgery of every day. Even Sands fell into thought a little while on these occasions. We returned to the lines to water and feed. In the afternoon we exercised again. This was the manner of our living those first weeks.

When you went by the guard at Mena House, and turned to the left to strike the long road to Cairo, you passed in a moment from sandy ways into the arms of a passionate throng gathered outside the gates. It needed a man of purpose to reach his goal undeterred. Brown, frantic faces closed in; gorgeous robes flowed before your eyes. Guides, donkeymen, camel drivers, money changers, fruit sellers, sweet sellers, motor drivers, beggars, fortune tellers, stamp dealers, postcard vendors, cigarette sellers, curio sellers, silk and cloth merchants—one and all screamed and pulled at you for patronage. Restaurant price lists, advertisements of hot baths or addresses of friendly ladies fluttered in your face. You were pulled to the nearest donkey, you were pushed to the nearest camel; a gharri backed into your path, and a motor hooted beside you. It was "This way, Australia! Australia very good, very nice! Oringies five one piastre! Nessles chocolate two piastres! Donkey, sir! Camel, very good, very nice!" And on your part it was, "Go to blazes, the lot of you!" The tramcar alone kept a dignified silence, for it was oversure of patronage. It had no upper story; and those who were cheated of room inside, climbed atop and dangled their legs over those below. A shouting, singing, swearing company set off for the mysterious pleasures of the waiting city.

At last you found your way to gharri or motor, paid your fare, sank down inside; and with fierce cries and a cracking of the whip or a sounding of the horn, you moved to the outskirts of the throng. A last brown face looked over the side and screamed, last dirty arms were waved in your face, and in a moment interest in you died, and the gathering swooped upon new victims. Then you were leaving the waiting camels, and eating up the miles to the town.

All the way the road was filled with hurrying

soldiers—tramsful, gharrisful, carsful of them. They forked their legs over tiny donkeys, they rolled to and fro on camels. There were those also who walked; but in these early and wealthy days they were not many. We passed people on the return journey—army service waggons loaded up, platoons of infantry, peasants back from market, children driving home flocks of sheep and goats. Once I saw a solitary figure praying on a carpet by the wayside. The desert was behind. True, on either side of the way stretched sand; but peasants worked here, and presently the countryside would grow green with crop. Now and again canals cut up the ground, and from them wandered away irrigation schemes of ancient pattern, put in motion by a listless bullock at a waterwheel. Quite suddenly one left behind such relics of past days, and came on the fringe of Cairo.

Had you left camp towards evening it was dark by now, and the tall houses frowned down or stared with their lighted windows. In the streets two continents rubbed shoulders, and faces of all shades and dresses of many fashions came into the light of the lamps as you rattled by. In course of time there appeared a quarter with broad thoroughfares and handsome shops, and tall houses built in French style; and somewhere here the journey ended.

The town was full of soldiers—Australians, New Zealanders, and English Territorials. They owned the place. They swaggered, hurried, or mooched down every street, stared into every shop, and commonly explored the inside. At all corners they were meeting and calling out; every dozen paces they pulled up to examine the wares of native merchants. No article hawked through the streets was too useless to find a purchaser. The fellows were like children in their delight, and the majority were orderly and well behaved.

They invaded the eating houses and the cafés; and patronised with equal goodwill the best hotels and the lowest wine dens. Men sat at beflowered tables who scarce knew the use of a napkin. In their purchases they were no less large minded. If there were customers for charms and glass necklaces, there were those who bargained for Persian carpets.

When the calm stars overhead had turned somewhat farther in their courses, and the lusty diners below thought strange thoughts born of the wine they had passed over-freely, it was then that the darker places of the city beckoned, and did not beckon in vain.

You left this great lighted square, where wealth and propriety sat side by side, you followed the length of an ill-lit arcade, you turned one turning and then another, and, behold, you might have travelled a thousand miles. The streets had shrunk to ill-lit crooked lanes, homes of strange smells, strange cries, and vague flitting forms. The tall, dirty houses leaned over you, leaving no more than a strip of sky filled with stars, and that very far away. When you passed the flaring lights flickering in the windows, painted faces smiled at you and eager hands beckoned. Out of wineshops sounded the notes of cheap pianos, and you heard the noise of dancers' feet, and it might be watched their shadows tossed across the windows. The doorways were filled with soldiers and women and haggling native merchants; and men lurched out to threaten passers-by, or to be hurried from the scene by comrades. There came the roll of tom-toms, or the high notes of reedy pipes; and maybe in some den you caught a glimpse of two or three cross-legged players, and a brown woman jerking herself through the steps of a dance. At any of these places hands might be laid on your shoulders, and hot, haggard faces might peer invitingly into your own.

All the while the business of every day went forward, so that children played at hide and seek round your legs, men urged laden donkeys through the congregation, and bawled the virtues of their wares. Staling meat and butter and vegetables lay on the slabs of the shops, and vehement women bargained there for to-morrow's dinner. You were buffeted and jostled from turning to turning, and your senses were excited and sickened by sights and odours. The breath of the multitude was heavy in your face. The cool of night found no way down there.

But it was not in these streets the strangest happenings took place, nor was it during the first hours of dark. There were many lanes to be followed, there was much wine to be spilled ere you had learned all. First you drifted to the Bullring, where much was to be seen and done; then you passed to the Wazir, where fresh secrets might be discovered. And then you——. Dear sir, over the nuts and wine, come, listen to me.

CHAPTER VII

THE PASSING OF WINTER

Winter passed and spring followed, bearing in its arms fierce suns and weary scorching winds. The desert camp remained until we learned to hate the country that once had amused us. By day, and more rarely by night, we manœuvred in the desert, making ready for the task which was so tardy in arriving. The life was hard; but I did not find it barren of pleasure. Many a long gallop had I over the shining sands, when the sun was scarce awake. I have spent mornings perched on some observing station while the batteries came in and out of action, and the heliographs flashed and the flags wagged. The Colonel proved a good master, though impatient and abrupt of speech. He spurred from point to point with half a dozen of the Staff on his heels, or sat in some trench on a hilltop, looking over the country with keen eyes. Also I learned the ways of the adjutant, a quiet man with little to say. On horseback he, too, moved swiftly about his business, covering many miles in a morning's journeying.

Sands—Sands the marvellous—became a telephone expert, and was to be found anywhere haranguing the cable-cart men, or kneeling on the ground, ear glued to the receiver of a field telephone. His conversations were worth the listening. One he held at midnight in the desert. We had word of an attack by infantry, and Sands hurried to the telephone to call up Eaves at the next station. "Eaves! Hullo there! Eaves, I say! Oh, damn and blast the thing, it won't work! Message for you! Eaves, are you there? Can't you hear me, man? Are you deaf? Message for you. Infantry advancing——! I say, are you there, Eaves? Eaves, I say! Oh, blast! Oh, damn! Oh, how beastly! Eaves, answer me at once! Mr. Sands speaking. Eaves, do you want to go under arrest?" Eaves (walking up and down somewhere in the Libyan desert to keep warm): "This game's no good to a man' keepin' a bloke 'anging round 'ere all night doin' nothin'. If a relief don't come soon, I'm goin' 'ome."

Truly Sands was a man in a thousand: none like him for cool effrontery; none like him for ignoring rebuffs; none like him for going back on statements without turning a hair. He pulled me up in stables one fine evening.

"Lake, your horse is very poor. Is it getting the extra feed?"

"Yes, sir."

"Well, what's it doing now? Why isn't it eating?"

"I was waiting for the order, 'Feed,' sir."

"Oh, man, you're a fool. I told you to feed that horse all day long. Feed it at once!"

"I thought the other horses would get restive, sir."

"Don't answer me back! Feed it at once!"

Next day he swooped on me as I carried "The Director" his food.

"Lake," he screamed, "what are you doing there? Are you mad?"

"I'm going to feed my horse, sir, as you told me."

"Man, you must be mad! You'd have the whole line torn up! I thought you knew something about horses. Put down the bag this minute!"

With the coming of the hot winds the shrunken army of tourists, who had this season braved the seas, departed for more kindly climates; and as our own wealth had long since been squandered, the city showed a more sober countenance. On the contrary, the camp had much improved: now it boasted picture shows, eating houses, hair dressers, bookshops, and tailors. But it failed to parch the seeds of discontent. The army spoiled for war. There came news of the Turkish dash for the Canal, and our Field Artillery was held in readiness. Hope revived for a brief space. But the attack came to nothing, and we continued in our uneventful ways. The suns grew hotter, the winds fell on us more fiercely, the flies multiplied. Men went about their work with bitter hearts.

Between "Turn out" and "Cookhouse" Sands

bore down on me as I loitered in the lines. Unsuspicious of his intention, I let him approach.

"Lake," he said, "the Colonel is wanted at once at Divisional Artillery Headquarters. I want a man to find him now. You will do. He went over to the palm grove with Major Felix. Saddle up immediately. Tell the corporal to keep your tea. I am sorry, but I can't help it." Sands was polite on occasion.

With heavy heart I walked away to saddle up "The Director." It was goodbye to my chances of tea. Any hope of success in the errand was small. A hundred roadways ran through the palms. "The Director" looked mournfully at his lost nosebag and followed me cheerlessly to the end of the lines. There I mounted, and we travelled the gunpark. I picked up no news from the sentry, and turned to the palms; I touched "The Director" with the spurs, and he went away over the sands at a long, easy canter.

It neared the hour of sunset, and the desert sparkled and grew rosy in the lights of the dying sun. I dropped the reins on "The Director's" neck, and let care slip away. My ill-humour was departing. The desert was cool, wide, empty, and silent; and the good beast beneath me moved with faintest footbeats on the sands. Farther down leaned the sun and the desert grew more rosy. The camp was behind and its last sounds fainting. Now the palm grove was near at hand.

The sun fell over the forest of treetops, polishing them as a jeweller polishes emeralds; but there was not a breath of wind to move a leaf. I passed into the trees near the smaller village. The peasants had left their work, and the herds were gathered home; but a few children played among the trees, and I called out, "Saida!" They ran up screaming. One or two I knew—Hanifa, Fatma, and Habibi, the belle of all. They could tell me nothing of the Colonel, and I scanned vainly for hoofmarks on the sand. Presently I chose a middle road leading into the heart of the palms, where I could see some distance to either side. The chance of success was small; but what better course was there?

Within the grove was cultivated ground, so that the paths which ran in many directions were often of no width at all. All these bright patches of green had grown up since our coming. Soon I lost sight of the desert altogether—unless it was to catch a quick glimpse now and again through endless trees. The place was still, and filled fast with shadows. In time I checked "The Director" to a walk: speed was of no account; luck only could bring success. Never had I known the place so empty: no labourer bent over his cultivation; no driver led home his string of camels; no marketer belaboured his laden donkey. Nor was there a sign of the men I sought.

But the journey was not in vain. I had passed a couple of miles through the trees, when I caught sight of them all of a sudden. They crossed the border of the desert land, moving towards home. They rode side by side, and distance changed them to pigmies. I could only guess at them.

I turned at a right angle to cut them off. No path led that way; but I made one of my own; and now and then the vegetable patches suffered. Progress was slow, and they had passed beyond me when I struck the sand. I spurred "The Director" and cantered up behind.

The Major turned first, and next moment the Colonel looked back. I saluted, and he returned the salute.

"You are wanted at once, sir, at Divisional Artillery Headquarters."

He answered something quickly; something not complimentary to Divisional Artillery. We rode on without hurrying the pace much, the Colonel and Major together, I a few lengths in the rear. At the edge of the camp the Major saluted and crossed to his own lines; and we turned our horses for Artillery Headquarters. We passed some distance in silence at a fast walk. Then said the Colonel:

"I think we're away at last, Lake."

"Thank God, sir!" said I.

"Thank God!" said he.

Then he spoke again.

"Lake, now is the hour to say—how does it run?—'Behold, O Allah, I make a sacrifice unto thee.'"

We approached Divisional Artillery. Said the Colonel: "Here I make my sprint to show my willingness."

And we spurred over the last stretch of sand.

The afternoon had grown old when we formed

up in the desert for the last time—when we mounted and passed in column of route through the camp towards the Pyramids Road. News of our going passed like a fiery cross through the new contingents we left behind, and they ran up and crowded either side of the way, giving us good speed and their cheers. "The Director" threw about his ears, and started on his fourstep; but a reminder from the spurs set him thinking of other things. We clattered along the hardened way, nodding and waving freely to friends, and settling our seat on saddle or limber. Everywhere gay voices called out above the rattle of movement. "So long, Bill—so long, old man—give it 'em in good old Australian style!" "We'll be with you soon, Joe!" "What's that, Jack! Right-o—give the Kaiser one from me!" "Look out there with that blasted 'orse: what's a bloke's toes for? To be danced on?" "So long, chaps! So long!"

I looked to right and looked to left, glad I was seeing all for the last time. On the right stood a thriving town of tents; but on our near side the desert was bare as far as the palm groves. It was the desert of our arrival eighteen weeks before. A turn in the way, and we had left behind the tented area, were winding between the picture shows and native bazaars and eating-houses. The crowd thinned. At Mena House the guard fell in to present arms; and next, before one could count ten, we were turning to the left hand, and streaming on to the road to Cairo. The desert was left behind.

At the corner was the usual ravening throng of guides, camels, donkeys, money changers, fruit sellers, carriage drivers, and touts. There was the usual native policeman to salute and smile. There was the usual rush of a dozen men with their wares, and the usual sideplay of nervous horses. Then we were beyond the tumult and into the quiet, sweeping along endless road, where two lines of trees held out their arms.

I pulled my gear into shape—I was half choked with baggage. Over a shoulder I stared at the Pyramids. The sun had climbed down into the sky, and now tossed immense shadows over the country. His beams were soft and bright. I rose in my stirrups to gaze a long while at the wonderful masses of stone. They stood as they had stood at our coming; and still they possessed the same power to awe me. From them I turned abruptly, and set my face down the road. The Colonel was looking backwards towards the camp. He, too, turned just then. "I never want to see that place again!" he burst out.

We had started in good time, and there was no hurry. The end of the column was not yet in sight. Ahead, the road was nearly deserted—a country lane in traffic though a thoroughfare in width. The months had brought great change. We kept to the right, unless a passing tram sent some of the horses across the way. Once a dozen Army Service waggons rattled by with forage aboard; and sometimes there were evil-eyed camels to pass, and strings of native cattle and flocks of shorn sheep, herded by glad-faced children. Sometimes a motor car tore out of the distance. But these meetings were far between on the long road.

"March easy" was blown, and caused at once a pulling out of pipes and cigarettes, and a quickening in the eye of cadgers as they singled out new victims. Hawkins rode beside me. Back down the lines trotted the trumpeter in time for a cigarette. He stuck it in the corner of his mouth, and winked at me. "Hail, most noble one, thou erstwhile bum Piccadilly-promenader! Sallyest thou forth to the field of battle?" He broke off to snatch the match from Hawkins's hands and light his cigarette. Drawing a deep glow, he threw his chest out and struck himself with a noble gesture. "I shall away to mine post in the van. Farewell, most valiant sirs!"

Peasants were at their work on both sides. They stayed their reaping and their watering to watch our passage; they fell to chattering among themselves, and to laughing. They were as light-hearted as we. The column continued at a walk, so that men would shoot a glance towards the officers, and all being clear, would break rank and trot up or drop back to some particular friend. All over the place one heard the same appeals. "Give us a cigarette, old man. Not 'ad a smoke all day." "I say, old chap, have you a match?" Or, "Where the 'ell do yer think you're going with that 'orse? Let 'is mouth go! Of course, 'e won't stand with you jerking 'is teeth out!"

The clatter of thousands of hoofs and the murmur of many hundred tongues set me pondering how soon this imposing train would be mouldering in the earth. A month hence, how many empty saddles would there be? How many riders mourning their steeds?

"Gunner Lake, Gunner Lake, peace to your unquiet thoughts. Verily you are no soldier. The good soldier performs what lies ahead: the good soldier does not think."

Shadows deepened; evening drew in; the sun set; the miles were eaten up. We had not halted. Of a sudden the country ended, and we were clattering through the suburbs.

The clamour of our going sounded bravely along the harder roads, and echoed into the gardens of private houses and into the upper apartments. Pale faces, olive faces, brown faces peered from windows, and over balcony rails: heads with hair piled high in French fashion, heads supporting pigtails bound with broad bows; heads crowned with red fezes. Heads of raven hair I saw, heads of brown hair, heads of silver. Many a smile the girls sent us; but the old men looked on without giving sign. Thus forward we went, and the traffic in our path had to bunch itself on the side of the way. The road ran on between the rows of houses: the houses seemed to have no end; and it grew darker and darker, until there were only seen dim forms on either hand and lights through countless windows.

An order came down from the head of the

column. "Halt!" At once there was tightening of reins, and the drivers lifted their short whips in the air. You could see the signal passing down the line. "Prepare to dismount!" "Dismount!" "Look round your horses!" I pushed my fingers under "The Director's" belly. He was hot and steamy, but quite well. I gave him a smack and left him.

Those who could, found seats on the curbstones, and started to munch chocolate or biscuits or whatever they had. But the rest was not for long. "Prepare to mount!" "Mount!" and in five minutes we were off again.

We came to a noble bridge bearing great lamps overhead. Beneath us flowed the ancient Nile. Countless native boats lay along the shores, and the lights from the city followed the moving waters as far as the eye could go. This was the river which had rocked Moses; the barge of Cleopatra had floated here; and now across it streamed a swollen foolish company, big with relief it was to write a word in the book of history. Which first shall be forgotten—Anzac, or the ancient, ageless Nile?

It was long dark when we came into the town proper, and neared the railway station. This way and that way we flowed through the twisted lighted streets, bringing the girls to the windows again, and the shopkeepers to their doors. The better quarters we did not see; for we followed back streets haunted by strange cries and stranger smells. Half the shops were eating-houses, where natives smoked together, drinking coffee, playing dominoes and backgammon. They would look from their square of light, and peer at us threading the outside dark. I do not think the blessings of Allah followed us every time.

We swept out of these places later on, into European parts. There came in sight a business quarter, hedged by brick walls with narrow lanes abutting. Here we joined other bodies of troops moving for like destination. Above the jangle and clatter sounded the whistles of engines and the bumping of trains. All at once we passed under a gateway, and came beneath the shadow of the station.

We—or the head of the column, that is—clattered into the courtyard and offsaddled. In no time the place was crowded with men and horses and vehicles. The square was in deep gloom, so that chaos took charge. I made out a long water-trough against a wall; I felt cobbles under my feet; there were tall buildings closing us in; and in a wall a lit-up window which might have been a ticket office, for I saw a man and a woman looking in there with luggage about them, and an hotel porter lolling by. There seemed two entrances to the square, one dim, leading from the streets, and one lit by an overhead lamp, where a ramp ran up from the yard on to the station platform. I received a hazy idea of all this ere the whirlpool caught me.

Men hurried this way and that; men shouted to one another, and cried out orders and swore; horses stamped and bumped and sidestepped. In truth it was no spot for a dreamer. Now, and again now, went up the cries, "Gangway there, gangway!" or "Clear the way!" and rattling and jangling a fearful warning to careless toes, a gun or limber manhandled rolled by towards the platform and the trucks. The Staff woke up to find itself pushed along the edges of the courtyard, some men holding three or four horses, and going through a pretence of hand-rubbing. Others discovered themselves unstrapping nosebags to push over tossing heads, or packing saddles in grain bags brought for that purpose.

The night became very close—and the steam from the horses, the odours of manure, and the personal discomfort occasioned by pushing about in the jumble of animals under weight of full marching order did not ease matters. Every few seconds some cross-grained four-legged brute would swing round or crush up; and it was *sauve qui peut* with a vengeance. All over the place showed Sands like the demon in a pantomime, ordering, expostulating, and reviling; and doing his best to survive sword, revolver, haversack, and the other impedimenta which trapped his movements.

"What are you doing standing there, Oxbridge? You're as useless as you are long! Lake, you're the slowest man in Egypt! Hurry, man, hurry! I told you not to pack those saddles that way, Eaves! You are the stupidest man I know. Oh, how damnable! How perfectly damnable!" And then he would disappear in a riot of horses, and someone would mutter, "I hope he's done in this time!"

The slender patience of the Staff failed under trial. Out of the darkness rose a voice.

"A bloke ought ter get six months for coming on a fool's game like this! Do they think a man's a dirty nigger all his life? Yer don't catch me 'ere again. Blast the Empire, I say."

"Fer Gawd's sake, shut yer row!"

"I won't shut it."

Then there went up a third voice. "You great, clumsy, awkward son of the devil; can't you let a cove's toes alone?"

This watering, feeding, and manœuvring of horses took a long while; but once all the nose-bags were properly fastened, the storm grew calm. But it was hard work still bending in the steamy night to force two or three saddles into a bag too small for them. I was glad enough to escape in time to the platform on some business or other. Hurry and confusion might be found there; but the place was lit up, which helped much, and there were no horses, which helped more. The train was drawn up to the platform—coaches for the troops in front, horse-boxes next, trucks for guns and waggons in the rear. The platform was in military hands, except in an out-of-the-way corner where two girls said goodbye to a sergeant. Already the trucks were loading: on one I found our telephone waggon, and farther down men hauled the cook's waggon aboard.

The place was as busy as an anthill on a sunny morning and as noisy as a rookery at even. Gangs of men swept to and fro, bearing baggage on their shoulders. Gangs of men hauled vehicles aboard the trucks, with cheery and weary cries and yo-hos. Still other gangs, roaring warning, pulled and pushed more vehicles up the ramp and rattled them at dangerous speed along the platform. Officers stood at fixed points to wave hands and direct; and sergeants and anxious corporals gave rest to none. Many a grumbler threatened below his breath; many a knowing hand vanished to the refreshment bar without leaving an address.

There were shrieks of engines, and much jolting and jarring, and endless snorting of steam. An engine was in process of coupling with our train. Before long a chain of our fellows came in view with the bagged saddles on their shoulders; and behind followed a line of horses for the trucks. Too late I saw them. I was seized to lend a hand. Nor was the office a sinecure; and I played the acrobat more than once keeping clear of all the heels.

We had arrived at the station in good time; but when I looked at the clock, the hour had grown late. Much remained to be done. Nearly all the horses were aboard, and all the heavy waggons; but quantities of lesser luggage arrived each minute on the backs of blaspheming men; nor did the stream show sign of running shallow.

But I had not long to look about: there were a thousand errands given me. Once I passed outside again, and found the courtyard blocked yet with traffic of waiting men and horses. I came back by the station buffet, where knowing ones drank coffee and ate such stale pastry as soldiers only buy. On the platform I ran into the Staff trucking the last horses, and must help again at the business. Luck smiled not this night.

Trucking and baggage loading finished together —our part of it, anyhow—and straightway we of the Staff were fallen in for a roll call. Three times was the roll run over before all were present.

It looked as though we should have breathing space at last, and I found I was hungry and borrowed a couple of shillings. But there was no chance of feasting. The hour of departure approached. There were signs of it everywhere. The platform did not empty of people; but men stood about in groups and drew arms across foreheads and flipped the perspiration on to the ground. No further space of freedom was given us. "Right turn! Left wheel! Quick march!" and away we went towards our carriage in the train.

"Aboard there, aboard," came the order.

We scrambled and pushed through the narrow doorway like schoolboys. The carriage proved a second-class undivided place, not overclean. The odour of natives clung to it yet. There was a scramble for seats. I was left one near the centre of the carriage, under a dingy light, but close to a window looking out on things. The men began to rid themselves of the marching gear which weighed as the nether millstone. There were seats for all, and there was little room for any. Thus started anew perennial argument. By the time gear was stacked we were no better than sardines.

This business of settling took time; and events must have moved rapidly on the platform, for without warning Sands himself appeared on a final tour of inspection, to tell us the train started in a few minutes, and to threaten anyone leaving the apartment with immediate arrest. Then he went away to his own carriage.

A man with ancient pastry put his head in at the door, and loud bargaining and a good deal of pushing was the order of the moment. The clamour still went on as a whistle sounded: on the first whistle came a second; and then arose the noise of lifted breaks, of turning wheels; and there followed a jerk and other jerks—behold, we were moving into the dark, and the station was falling behind. Far abroad went a cheer, while a hundred arms waved from the windows: and then we had drawn out of the station and were jolting through the night.

There followed immediately on all this tumult some strange moments of pause, as though the knowledge had fallen on us that we were starting a journey which would be the last for many good fellows. But those moments were no more than moments, and men began to find their seats, to overlook their gear again and even to get supper out. At the end of five minutes a noisy order reigned. We were bumping through the town, and I looked from the window to see lights come and go; and to catch odd scenes, such as a house set in a garden of palms, a level crossing where waited a native and his camel in lazy patience; a glimpse of water flecked with the images of stars.

From the town we passed to the suburbs, always gaining speed; we left the suburbs behind and drew into flat open country. Here were no lights for guidance, and the night was dark. I could make out little of what passed; but here and there shadows pointed to the sky, and vague huts and hamlets sped into the square of light and out again.

But I tired soon enough and instead got ready supper. We had our iron rations, that was all—tins of bully beef and biscuits—only I had remembered a last tin of sardines, and I fared well. We loitered over supper, and afterwards many started to gamble, and as many went off to sleep. Apart from the arguments of the card-players, there was little talking done: nobody talked for talking's sake. The train rumbled on through the night, until it might have travelled all Africa. I found myself yawning. I was cramped, especially about the legs; but it is an uneasy seat that stops the old dog sleeping. I began to yawn and lay back, and soon I was drowsy, and next I nodded. Farther and farther through the night jerked and clanged the train; and I would start to life and see the rowdy gamblers, and the other men who dozed like myself. Next anew in drowsiness I sank. At last I must have fallen asleep.

As the stars paled before a cheerless dawn and circulation and spirit were at lowest ebb, the train drew up and emptied us on to the platform of Alexandria. Such is a soldier's fortune.

There were last night's doings to repeat. We stumbled on to the platform, bag and baggage, to be fallen in without ado. The roll was called. On all horizons the sky was cold and grey, and last stars faded in it. Yet while we stood there, looking sleepily up, faint colour crept into the East, and grew with the minutes, painting a picture of a forest of masts and a score of great sails of native boats. But this was not an hour of admiration. "'Shun! Right turn! Quick march!" was our portion, and away the gallant band marched to untruck horses, to gather up saddles and other gear, to perform endless fatigues. Daylight was abroad long before we finished. Then there remained watering and feeding—but no talk of breakfast for us.

The harbour was filled with transports, and many ships stood out to sea. All signs were here of a mighty expedition. From train to wharf where lay our boat was short distance, and all things were collected there at last.

The transport was a-hum with business. Cranes screamed and rattled, and men swarmed the decks, or ran up and down the gangways. She was the s.s. *Hindoo*, a good-looking vessel. Already she was three parts loaded, and she would sail that night. The wharf where she lay was blocked past belief with horses, guns, and limbers and all the baggage of war. Left of us, a French mule corps had collected; and past it was a French airship transport corps.

But why recall that day? We were loaded by evening, and about our ears fell the rattling of the dripping anchors. I stood on deck above the emptying wharf. And the Colonel passing by said, "We are off, Lake." Foot by foot we drew out from land: fathom by fathom widened the band of water. In middle harbour we turned about, and steamed to the open sea. The lights of land went out: Africa was no more. The screw thumped and churned, and we moved into the ocean towards an unknown anchorage.

CHAPTER VIII

MUDROS

It seemed at last we were drawing into port. The land was more defined, and rolled up from the sea in peaceful grassy slopes, chequered with squares of cultivation, and marked with lonely dots which later might grow into hamlet or farm. Nearer—always nearer—the ship steered, until the waterway had narrowed to a ribbon, and the island discovered itself entirely, presenting cliffs which swept into the water, and beaches shelving smoothly down. Caressing breezes came over to us, like breaths from a promised land.

We could not name the place. Scores of faces watched the approaching hills, scores of tongues cried out where we had arrived. Many declared for the Dardanelles; as many for Tenedos; as many for Lemnos; but it remained to watch and wait. Finally we were moving parallel with the shore, towards a cape directly ahead—everywhere the gentle slopes climbed up towards the hills, carrying vegetation all the way. Sunbeams flecked the pasture land, and swept across the squares of cultivation. Balmy breezes floated to us anew.

We steered beyond the cape, and two great jaws of land opened wide. Inwards we steamed. And behold, the spell was shattered. Again our cries broke out.

We were entering a large and sheltered bay, where the same green hills climbed from the sea, the same patches of cultivation marked the easier slopes, and the same hamlets clustered in the shelter of the valleys. But these things had not loosed our tongues.

A mighty fleet lay at anchor in the land-locked waters—two fleets indeed: a battle fleet, and a fleet of transports. It was a wondrous spectacle to come across by an out-of-the-world shore. Across the mouth of the bay had been drawn a net, past which no enemy submarine might find passage; and beyond the net anchored in safety all these craft of war. Grim battleships lay there, and swift cruisers with sunlight slipping over their grey sides. Low black destroyers found place beside them; and a submarine, half submerged, with the crew upon the conning tower, and the sea climbing to right and left out of her path, passed down the thoroughfare. Trawlers, tug-boats, colliers, lighters, mine-sweepers—all that can be named were anchored before us; and giant liners swayed their cables and showed decks crammed with uniformed men.

Noble was that company, and one there was nobler than all. Long and low and plain of detail, the *Queen Elizabeth* nursed jealously her fifteen-inch guns. Through the lines she moved now: she passed the open net into the outer bay: she gathered speed and churned towards the Dardanelles. Only a broad wake remained as signal of her passage.

In such way we arrived in Mudros Harbour and took our place in the waiting company.

On one another's heels the days went by, and still we lay at anchor in the sheltered waters, impatience growing with each rumour and fresh delay. New transports continued to arrive, whereby daily the bay became more crowded; and there were reports of yet more transports on the way. We were to weigh anchor to-morrow. Now we were remaining for a fortnight. Now Turkey discussed terms of peace and we would not be wanted. Such rumours were born each morning. Each day saw a like programme performed—stables, stables, and again stables. Grumbling flourished as the green bay tree.

I was not the quietest of the growlers—yet, even so, I never quite shook off the glamour of that island set in the Aegean. Never was there an early morning when skies were not blue and waters unruffled. Breezes softer and more scented than any human kisses floated perpetually to us from the green hills. Every sunrise brought the same brisk scene, when gigs, cutters, and small boats of a hundred designs plied between the giant ships. Against our sides bumboats would presently collect, handled by wily Greeks with offerings of tobacco, dried fruits and nuts, or

Turkish delight and chocolate. Business was always brisk until whisky arrived abroad, and afterwards the bumboats came no more. Aye, the magic of those mornings stays with me.

There were days when the battleships left the anchorage: and the smaller craft, such as the destroyers, were active at all hours. Hither and thither through the lines they moved at speed, coming and going on their journeyings. Many a time I wondered over their business.

But if the mornings could discover fairyland, the nights knew the secret no less. Many an evening the sun went down behind shadowy hills which circled a bay of glass, whereon destroyers had ceased to manœuvre and last rowing boats were putting home. While the deeper shadows found a road over the water, it might be a belated submarine churned by, conning tower a-wash, like a strange monster of the deep.

Then the day's work was over, and men gathered on deck for the breezes which revived about this hour, or settled below to gamble until "Lights out" was blown. The hills would retreat, the water would turn to formless grey, and the great boats would give up their shape. The stars would look out; and to rival them, a thousand lanterns shone forth upon the waters. Far into the night—all through it, I vouch—winked the Morse lights. "Dot, dash, dot: dot, dot, dash."

When evening aged, and man's energy had revived, we held sing-songs on the deck below the bridge. No bright peculiar star illumined the meetings; but Time passed by on lighter foot. B Battery had a song by a poet of theirs, which always scored encores. It ran like this:

> We are the boys of this good Batterie,
> The joy and the pride of the Artillerie;
> We do not like work; but what soldiers do?
> And we're after the Turk on the good ship *Hindoo.*

Later on men appeared with their bedding—a blanket and a rug, with a coat for pillow—something of that sort—and put it down in unoccupied spaces. The groups about the piano would thin, before ten o'clock lights on the troopdeck went out, the men turned into bed, and conversation died to whispers. So another day of waiting ended. Often I would lie awake to stare up at the chilly stars, or to watch the tireless winking of the Morse lights. At those times many a strange thought knocked at the doors of my brain.

At last it seemed our waiting was over. Rumour became persistent and less vague. Something of the plan of campaign was told us, and we were detailed to our boats and our duties. I was given a place in the first boat leaving the ship, as Colonel's orderly. I took heart from that moment.

The plan of attack was in this manner. The Frenchmen were to land at Kum Kale on the Asiatic side; the British at Sed-el-Bahr opposite. The New Zealanders and ourselves would pass beyond the British, and attempt a point somewhere near Gaba Tepeh. A fleet of mine-sweepers was the van of the expedition, with cruisers to follow and cover the destroyers bearing the infantry. Behind came the artillery, behind them yet other units. The approach would be made by night, and the attack launched at break of day. The artillery transports carried two batteries from one brigade, and a single battery from another, with the idea that two boats might unload together, and a complete brigade be put ashore in record time. All horses would remain on board a day or two at least. Such meagre details we received; but we were told everything had been considered, and the undertaking would prove among the greatest of history.

Finally arrived the afternoon of the last day.

Through the morning there had seemed no unusual preparation: indeed the lively destroyers were drawn up in a little fleet on one side, where they steamed idly all day. With declining afternoon there came a rattling of our anchor cables and a general business of seamen, and later the murmurings of turning screws: and, before it might be realised, our boat was swinging and moving down that populous thoroughfare towards the open sea. Up went a burst of voices, up and across the bay; and to starboard and to port of us decks filled with khakied men. Solemnly we moved along. Many a noble craft of war we passed, with cold grey sides and polished guns; many a splendid liner bearing a townshipful of men. Past all we went—past all—and through the open net into the outer bay. Our engines slowed again, cables roared and rattled anew, and the anchors plunged into the sea. Here we must wait until the final hour.

We were of the earliest transports to move. Now the fleet followed us in single procession. Some anchored in our neighbourhood, many steamed on towards the horizon; there seemed no rule. The sun sank down, and ocean and skyline met in a clear rim; and where they met, tiny black cruisers were silhouetted against the light. They were to guard us through the night.

The sun rim was a-dip. Close to starboard of us had anchored a French trooper, and now about her clustered a weird fleet of pinnaces, towing chains of open boats. We were wondering at the meaning of the sight when word arrived that the Frenchmen would practise a landing. The boats filled with men, the signal was given, the pinnaces steamed at speed for the shore. Like hurrying serpents they swept through the oily waters to meet the land as dusk descended.

Against the glowing sky I noted the heads of the men moving above their huddled bodies, and the thin rifle barrels bristling everywhere. One could not see the faces, one could only imagine; yet I know the uneasy and the stern were there; and those who called on One mightier than themselves to help them through the morrow.

Down went the sun: upon the ocean lamps came out, and lamps came out in the sky. The green and red lights of the hospital ships glittered like fairy palaces. All evening, and into the night, boats threaded the way out of harbour. The hours went by. "Lights out" was blown. Upon the quiet ocean a navy and an army rested. Yet maybe one or two forms stayed restless, dreaming of the dawn.

I was on stable picket. About seven o'clock I carried my blankets down on to the horse deck, and laid them out on the hatchway between the bales of lucerne. The hatch above was open, so that I could look straight up into the sky; but even then the air was close and musty, for there was little wind abroad and none found a way down here. The horses moved wearily in the stalls, rattling head-chains and stamping impatiently. They were as tired of the voyage as ourselves. Now one rubbed itself endlessly against the bars of the stall, now a mare snapped spitefully at a neighbour. Everywhere dwelt the musty odour of manure and hay.

The other pickets sat by their lines, and talked and smoked, and kept an eye on the companion for the orderly officer. I walked up and down, patting some of the horses and calling out to the biters and kickers. I felt as restless as the worst of them. All my thoughts were of the morning. Presently I sat on a bale of lucerne, and dropped my chin on to my hands. Still went on the rattling of chains and the shuffling of feet. But away from it all I travelled at last.

The horse deck was practically dark in places, for there was a single electric lamp hanging low over the hatchway for every man to knock himself against, or stumble over with an oath. It would be better later on. The stars shone lustily through the open, and soon there would be part of a moon. My thoughts travelled further and further from the present, until the horses and their ill-temper were forgotten.

There came steps down the companion. The pickets sprang to their feet, hid the cigarettes and paced up and down. The alarm was false. Mr. Campbell arrived to look at his mare. He came round to where I sat, patted her shoulder, and started to call her pet names. Then he saw me.

"Good evening, Lake," he said. "I came along to have a look at 'Bonnie.'"

"Have you any news to give, sir?" I said.

"Yes. We leave here at midnight. At four o'clock we pass the French landing, and at five we shall see the British. We are going some distance beyond them. The infantry have started already."

"Thank God we're making a move at last," I said.

"Yes, Lake," was his answer, and he laughed. There followed a little pause, and then he said, "Good night, Lake," and went up the companion.

I sat down again on the bale. I was surprised to find how fast the time had gone, for my relief arrived a few minutes later. We talked for more than half an hour, and then I turned into bed. I rolled up in the blankets and started to read. I was directly under the light, and I had a magazine to finish. I read and read, feeling utterly unlike sleep. I read until I yawned my head off. The heavy air and monotonous noises made me drowsy, and still I could not sleep.

The picket that had relieved me was relieved in his turn. The magazine was finished. I threw it aside and lay back, yet I felt less like sleep than ever. Overhead the stars had circled half-way round the sky. They were less bright, so I knew the moon had come up. Surely it must be midnight, said I.

Just then there came much movement overhead, and a turning of winches and a roaring of cables, and I knew we weighed anchor for the last time. Up jumped the pickets crying, "We're off, boys, we're off"—and one ran up the ladder like a monkey and climbed on to the upper deck. Presently he poked his head down into the light. "We're off all right: it's dinkum this time!" The screws began to turn, and the boat began very gently to throb. The movement woke up the horses and set them shuffling in the stalls, rattling with new energy the head-chains. I lay on the broad of my back and stared straight up.

"Gunner Lake, Gunner Lake, beyond those lights Azrael arises and spreads out his wings. At dawn he flies wide for his harvest, to return at even with much booty. The merry of to-day will be with him, and the downhearted; the blasphemous and the pure will be there: here and there he will have flown, picking up without choice and design. Aye, Gunner Lake, even you may be of that silent company. Is that why you toss here to-night, and woo sleep so vainly? Go, rest—what matters it? Let the Book of Death be opened wide; and be your name writ there, add to it a bold AMEN."

CHAPTER IX

THE LANDING IN GALLIPOLI

I ENDED by waking up quite late in the morning—not only ended by waking up late, in fact, but even by forgetting the undertaking ahead of us. I discovered myself on my back, looking through the open hatchway at the sky, where a pleasant breeze found a way down, and drove off the musty odours of manure and pressed lucerne. For half a minute maybe I lay thus, thinking of nothing much, and hearing in a far-off way the shuffling of the horses. Then of a sudden the business before us came into my brain like a thunderclap; and I read a fresh meaning into the scene. Daylight had crept nearly over the sky, and the deck above was full of men come up for the morning wash, with towels about their necks and soap in their hands. Instead of washing, all looked in one direction. The landing, of course.

Up went my head, and I listened hard for the guns, but not a sound I caught. I did not wait long after that. In three minutes my toilet was finished, and up the ladder two rungs at a time

I went, to find myself on the hatch top and a big crowd of fellows all round me.

The first thing I noticed was the stiff breeze. The air was full of salt. I slid down from the uncertain perch into the crowd, and made a way to the rail. Considering the breeze the sea moved very little, and the weather gave promise of becoming fine and clear. However, it was not light enough to see properly the horizon, and after a long look round I had distinguished nothing. I came across Wilkinson and Lancashire.

"Can you see anything?" I said. "I can't see a thing or hear a damned thing either."

"No, there's nothing doing yet," they answered.

"I thought we were to pass the French about four o'clock?"

"We did pass them a long time ago, but too far out. They're looking for the English landing now; but I heard a bloke say we wouldn't pass it before breakfast."

I went on to the troop deck after that, for a towel and soap. There were still a good many fellows rolled up in the hammocks or on the floor or the mess tables. Any who were awake called out to know what was going on, and hearing nothing, settled down to another ten minutes. I had my wash and a hairbrush, and next went to the parade deck, and stayed leaning over the rails listening for the guns until the trumpeter blew "Stables."

For an hour we were in stables doing the usual

things; and I think affairs went less wearily. On the way to breakfast not a man did not linger to discover what might be seen or heard; but no sign or sound of battle did we obtain. The sea rolled away on every side, as it had done a score of mornings before; and now the horizon was quite clear, and proved void of battleships or any craft at all.

I forget what there was for breakfast. It was curry, I think. I know there was less of a scramble than usual, as a number of fellows stayed above hoping to see something, and others were excited and off their appetite. For my part I filled up well, not being overcertain of the next meal, and when I could tackle no more I went straight up on deck again.

All along the starboard side of the boat fellows were hanging over the rails: there was a great crowd of them, half the boat's company at least. I edged a way in among them, asking what was doing. "Can't you hear the guns?" someone said. And nobody said anything else.

There was absolutely nothing to be seen, so I put my head on one side and listened. Beyond the breathing and coughing of the others, the many noises of the vessel and the shifting of the seas, I distinguished nothing, certainly no sound of guns; and then all at once I picked it up, and afterwards never lost it. It was faint, faint, ever so far away, an endless, tireless grumbling or murmuring. I drank the sound rather than heard it. It was like a draught of thunder and champagne.

Fresh fellows came up from breakfast, and pressed behind us. Some would cry out and some say nothing, according to their nature; but, all considered, it was a sober gathering. Aye, and there was reason, too. Three hours, four hours on, and some of us would have started a journey where the echo of those guns might not follow.

I stayed on and on there, and nobody else seemed to go away. The while that firing grew more distinct, until it was no more a muttering, but had become a sullen, weariless booming, soaring up and down, a booming with the power to intoxicate the heart. I listened with soberness befitting a guest at one of Death's At Homes; and yet I was ready to shout too, shout that I was coming, that soon I would be there.

We had kept a fair speed all the way; but now methought we slowed somewhat, as though it might be we were ahead of time. The other transports closed a fraction, and we drew up with two boats ahead, and thus, somewhat bunched, steamed towards the menacing horizon.

At last our watching was rewarded. Out of the horizon drifted the battle.

There climbed into the sky what seemed a barren mountainous land, and where this country gathered in a headland of some prominence a number of boats lay out at sea. They were no more than dots upon the water. It was the fleet.

Now the gunfire was distinct and threatening,

like—I don't know what it was like, I can't find words—but a grander and more awful sound I had not heard.

The battle came towards us, and we must have travelled faster than I believed, for very soon afterwards the fleet had taken shape, and next we saw the shells shatter in vast dust clouds on the heights. The solemn roll of the guns was no more. It had grown into a series of thunderous broken explosions. Now the flashes showed, and now we could distinguish the battleships from the transports close in shore. Now we found the water dotted over with mine-sweepers and tugs, and Heaven knows what else besides! Captive to one of these tugs, and well out to sea, hung high up a staring yellow balloon. They were "spotting" from it.

At first we had seemed to be steering directly for the centre of battle; but now it was evident we would pass far to the left hand. We were drawing into the medley of small craft whose duty was over, and now waited on the outskirts of the fray. Farthest of all from danger was the big yellow balloon, and in time we came nearly under it, and I threw back my head and stared up, envying the man there with his telescopes.

For on deck one could really see very little. The land did not seem far off, and yet it must have been miles away, for one could make out nothing beyond the outline of the battleships, and the great shell-bursts on the ridges: no sign of men or targets, nothing of that sort. The gunflashes, the smoke clouds, and the voices of the explosions were endless and very distinct, for now we were level with the point, and about as near as we should ever be. For some time our speed had lessened a good deal, but even so we made good headway, as very soon the battle had fallen behind, and we were drawing out of the crowded waters. The gunfire died into the old endless roll, and once again we were left listening and looking at one another.

The coast ran on and on along our starboard side, and all the way appeared the same mountainous barren land. The morning had turned out duller than it promised: there were patches of sunshine and patches of cloud, and a dullness along the horizon hinting at rain later on. I believe we slowed still more after this. We seemed only to drift forward. And then the trumpeter blew "Stables."

Nobody showed readiness to go below and sweat among the horses; but before long we were jostling one another down the companion, and next starting at the old game of rolling out the mats and exercising. The hatches of the hold were open, for fellows were down below fusing shells, and loading up the waggons; and this cramped us for room more than ever, and added a risk into the bargain.

Now as morning wore on, the rumble of guns came down to us once more, and started us listening anew. Every minute brought the sounds with greater distinctness, until the even roll a second time broke into many separate explosions.

I should have liked to run up the ladder and find out what was going forward, but Mr. Gardiner stood at the bottom, and I resigned myself to follow on in the weary procession of men and horses.

Three or four of our fellows were on deck, hauling up by rope the baskets of manure as we filled them. All of a sudden there was no reply to our tuggings and oaths, and at last a man went up to find out what was the matter. The messenger himself disappeared for three or four minutes, and then the whole party turned up suddenly to look over the hatch side and cry out that there was a bonza affair going on ahead. Several men threw over what they were doing and sneaked away, and in a few minutes' time Mr. Gardiner himself went off, leaving us alone. After that I decided to have a look on my own account. I had just put back my horse, and up the ladder I went and stepped on to deck.

There were a good many fellows about, all staring ahead. We were coming into another battle, only we were nearer into land this time, so that the vegetation could be made out; also there seemed more craft engaged or standing by, and the shell-bursts were splashing on the hills in the merriest manner. Even now we were several miles removed from matters, and, looking over the side, one seemed almost at a standstill. I could not stay long, as Mr. Gardiner might re-appear at any moment, so I dodged back again, and took out the next horse. But I need not have hurried. Gardiner had not returned, and most of the other fellows were gone. They straggled back one by one, talking with animation, and even laughing and calling out. We passed the news with sundry additions to the people sitting on the shells in the bowels of the ship; and before we had properly finished, Mr. Gardiner turned up again, and the slow machinery got into motion. For the next half-hour, next hour perhaps, the gunfire grew more distinct, until it was obvious the fight must be quite near at hand. In spite of—or perhaps because of—the general unrest of the Staff, every horse received full share of exercise, and towards midday there were still half a dozen animals to take out. However, I decided I had done enough for the morning. I edged behind the feed-bin, and at first chance went up the gangway. What I saw there kept me watching.

We had drifted right into the battle. I suppose we were lying two or three miles off shore, though it looked no distance over the water. The land was quite distinct. The mountains seemed to run right down to the water's edge, and were covered with vegetation—whether of size or not I could not tell—lying as closely as hairs sprout on a man's head. Several big valleys ran into and over those hills, as though inviting us to follow them along; but though the sun shone just now across the landscape, I was not particularly enamoured of it. No! an uncharitable land, said I.

As a matter of fact I had no time for the land at first; I could not leave the sea. The water teemed with boats, it floated a Noah's Ark of boats—two of every build. There were Dreadnoughts and there were rowing boats, and there was everything else between. Our place was rather at the back of affairs, among other transports and such non-fighting craft; but even round here was a waiting destroyer or two, stationary it might be but panting to be off, smoke wisps curling from the funnels, men at the posts on deck, and an officer at the bridge with glasses clapped to his eyes.

The armoured boats were at work singly, some lying miles off their targets: and at short and uneven intervals one or other would send out long spouts of flame from her turrets, half hide herself behind a roll of grey smoke, and then reappear. Over the water followed a rumble or boom or bellow, according to size of gun or distance, and on the hilltops three or four funnels of dust would go up. Some of the targets were over the ridges, beyond our sight altogether; but frequently shells fell this side upon the dull green crests. I warrant many a tragedy was happening over there; but all looked very calm and empty across the sliding waters. There seemed no order of firing: it was one boat here and one there. The explosions were not as continuous as earlier in the morning, and I wondered if the crisis of affairs were passed.

At first it seemed we were having all our own way; but in time I discovered the enemy answered back from somewhere right over the hills. While I watched, the sea received their efforts;

but in spite of this a feeling of uncertainty fluttered the spectator's heart, for the shells I saw plunging into the sea were of the kind one would not stroll into twice. A destroyer but a few cable lengths away had a waterspout over her bows; and she did not wait for the Turkish gunner to correct his range. Our fellows were as eager as at a football final, and laughed at the misses and called out when a bull's-eye was nearly scored. Before long I was hemmed in by a pushing, hard-breathing company.

I went down to the horse deck again. Gardiner was in his old place, and there was no difficulty in joining the crowd. The work was nearly over, men were putting back the last horses and mixing the feed. Quite soon came the order, "Turn out."

Things were still the same on deck. The weather had improved. The sun was bright and hot. I went on to the top deck, and found Hawkins and one or two others there, and we sat on a hatch top and watched the battle. It was Sunday; but instead of church bells, we listened to twelve-inch guns. One of the party who had glasses picked up a company of our infantry in the scrub on top of the hills. I thought probably he lied, for I saw nothing; but he spoke the truth, as presently on to a patch of open land came a number of puny figures, and ahead of them plumped our shells with gay precision. They crowded the open space in quick time, and next the scrub engulfed them. There was no sign of the enemy, who must have been retreating. The rest of our watching showed us nothing, the scrub telling no tales.

The battleships continued to range on to the hilltops and beyond them in a fairly busy manner and the enemy continued to answer. Once or twice the good ship *Hindoo* seemed to be a target, and I warrant a good many of us were set wondering where the next shell would fall; but none came aboard. We went on yarning and watching and calculating until "Cookhouse" went.

Tank had spent the morning flagwagging on the bridge. He was idle as our meeting broke up, and sat on the boards dangling his legs and looking at the battle. I went up and gave him a "Hallo." He looked down.

"Well, what do you think of things?" said I. He screwed up his mouth and shrugged his shoulders.

"Yes, Corporal," I went on, half in earnest and half in fun, looking into his face, "to-night a Tank or a Lake may lie spreadeagled over there."

He answered quite seriously in his funny, jerky manner, "I am not coming back. I saw it quite plainly a little while ago. We went over in a boat, a lot of us, and got to shore, and I was running up the beach, and was hit and fell back. I saw it as plain as anything." He was so serious he made me grin.

"I'm sorry to hear the news, Corporal," I said. "You didn't see me there by any chance?"

He looked at me in his sad way, and I could

not help feeling sorry for him. There was no reason for it. Tank always over-ate and so had liver, and consequently got the blues. Yet I was always a little sorry.

Thinking of Tank's liver reminded me "Cookhouse" had gone, and that I should go hungry unless I hurried. I went down to the mess deck, which hummed with life from end to end. Some ate at top speed, stretching over the tables for what they wanted and shovelling it into them. Others sat on the steam pipes round the room, putting together kits or cleaning rifles; and others yet hung out of portholes, and gave bulletins of the day.

I made a good dinner. The first boat left in a couple of hours, and this was the final meal on board. Afterwards I dumped my kit in a corner, put the rifle with it, and went on deck again.

All day the boat had seemed fuller than usual, everywhere there were crowds and to spare. The troop deck had overflowed with men, and now up here one had to thread a way about. Fellows still exclaimed and pointed whenever a shell dropped overnear; but on the whole the throng was quieter, though excited yet.

It was not long before Mr. Gardiner arrived and ordered those of the Staff detailed for landing to get into marching order. I girt myself with waterbottle and haversack, and hung the iron rations at my belt. There were a dozen other things about me too, and when I had pulled an overcoat over my shoulder and had taken hold of a rifle, I felt more ready for an armchair than an enemy to engage.

One or two of our fellows were on the parade deck ready for a final yarn, and I was not long pulling off my coat again and sitting down. We were not due to leave for two hours.

The crowding and bustling went on all the while, and the final hour came very fast. An empty barge was brought alongside and secured with hawsers, when it stayed to grate gently against us. A rope ladder was thrown over, and men went down and busied themselves making ready for the guns and limbers. There was more energy to-day than usual.

Norris had come on to the scene overloaded like myself. He and I were for the same boat, the first one. On his back was a box affair with a red cross on the lid. He came up to me where I stood craning over the side, watching the lowering of the guns and waggons. He said something, I've forgotten what. Nothing Norris said was ever of importance. Then someone whirled up to us and ordered us aboard the barge at once. I gathered all together, and with Norris pushed through the crowd to the rope-ladder. There were more people than ever just here, for the guns were going over, and the barge bobbed up and down, making their lowering no go-as-you-please affair. Orders and oaths were to be heard for the listening.

It was a good drop down to the barge—thirty foot, maybe—nor was the rope-ladder the easiest of stairways. With a prayer that Norris would not fall on my head, I pushed up to the side, climbed over the rails, and got hold of the ladder. I felt as nimble as a steamroller, and glanced uneasily on to the uncompromising objects below. The farther I went, the more the ladder swayed; but in the end things were managed, and I stowed myself into a corner of the barge. She was broad and stout, seeming very safe from shipwreck; but she lifted up and down on the choppy sea like a playful elephant.

The loading was over. Three or four perspiring men knelt among the gun wheels making final lashings, and later one by one straightened their backs and went up the ladder.

The other fellows on the Staff had gone down to stables, and now and then someone would poke a head through the portholes to see how matters went. Witty remarks passed between us, and I was making my best retort when the colonel and adjutant showed above, and came climbing down the ladder. They made room for themselves beside me, and the only man now missing was the doctor. We had "A" Battery guns aboard, and "A" Battery fellows with them, of course.

There had been plenty of sunshine through the day; but the weather still looked uncertain. The sky was high up and blue and clear, and heavy white and grey clouds chased across it. Little gusts of wind got up of a sudden and passed with as slender warning. I hoped hard the evening would prove charitable. I had small fancy for a wet skin.

We waited only for the doctor, and just now a naval launch steamed out of nowhere towards us. In charge was a junior lieutenant, who ran it alongside and called out in high-pitched tones to know if we were ready. He was a big fellow, young and fat, and very much at his ease. No doubt he had run the gauntlet of the shore several times already. He wore his second or third best clothes, and they and his broad back gave him something of a church-going look. His manner was very mild.

The launch cast aboard us a hawser, and we fastened ourselves to her ——, I have no nautical terms.

"Are you ready, sir?" called the heavy lieutenant.

"No," the colonel cried back. "The doctor's not here! Where's Doc?" he exclaimed impatiently to himself. "What's the matter with the fellow?"

Just then the doctor showed up above, and the colonel, who had cast a hundred glances that way during the last five minutes, shouted out, "Hurry up, Doc, hurry up, man! We're just off! You're late, man! You're late!"

The doctor came down the ladder as fast as he could, and half a dozen hands steadied him for the final drop. He was just aboard as the naval officer called out again, "If you're ready, sir, cast off from the ship, please!" We threw overboard our ropes; and the launch, which had chug-chugged fussily alongside, moved up ahead of us, strained on our hawser, and took us in tow. Now we were moving gently through the waters, and the great hull of the ship towered above, and the fellows in hundreds hung over the side and sent after us their best luck. Woods's black head looked through a porthole and gave me a couple of short nods, and I felt he envied me my seat. Then we were free from the ship and speeding briskly along. The sea was clearing of craft, and we turned towards the emptier ways. Next we had swung in our course and were steering towards the hills.

Now, as we passed into clearer waters, and the choppy waves splashed our sides, sending the clumsy barge bumping up and down, I drank a further draught of life's champagne. The officers and fellows sat quietly in their places, all looking to the land which was growing into shape. No doubt I sat as quiet as any, no doubt my own eyes seldom left the land; but the moment I had often thought of was come, and I found myself ready for it.

Forward we went towards the frowning anchorage, at the pace of a pleasure boat making for a picnic ground. Ten minutes, five minutes, and we should meet their rifle fire. Aye, there we sat in the horse barge, as still as still could be, some shielded by the guns and waggons, some bent forward and very solemn, but all, I warrant, thankful the hour had struck. In the launch a cable's length away every man was behind armour. The officer looked through a hole before him, and turned from time to time to the man at the spitting engine, or in spare moments examined the shape of his boots. The man at the engine was frowning and looking at the land.

We throbbed over the choppy waters, and the hills marched towards us, showing themselves full of ragged gulleys bristling with stunted scrub. Not a soldier moved among them, not a puff of smoke came out; but there was a roar of guns behind us, and there was a far-off bubbling sound ahead. I did not know what it meant then, I gave it small attention; but I was to learn its meaning well enough. Forward we went, and the band of waters narrowed, and a strip of sandy shore came out below the hills. Then high overhead passed a thin, singing sound, and the first bullet flicked the water yards away. We were within rifle range. "Get under cover, everyone!" somebody called out, and all who could dived down among the waggons. A second bullet went by and a third; but they passed high over, or to the right or left. But the sound was new and set me thinking.

We neared shore quickly now—half a mile of water was all that intervened. The beach was plainly to be seen as a narrow sandy stretch running as far as you like to right and left. And then I was surprised to find the whole flat crowded with people; and in places were stacks of stores in building, and straight before us was a wireless plant fully rigged. They were losing no time! And—Jove, yes!—there were sappers driving roads; and—Jove!—there was a mule battery passing from view.

As we bumped along, the one or two bullets

that passed our way, and an odd dose of shrapnel falling generally afar off, were all the attention the enemy gave us; but nearing the land, matters warmed up. Steady doses of shrapnel were coming over the hills. They were meant for the beach, no doubt; but the angle of descent was tricky, and nearly all overshot the mark and hissed into the water. To hear the clap overhead and the rush of bullets on to the waves made one start measuring the distance to the friendly cliffs. I was down between a waggon wheel and the barge's side, and, despite an uneasy feeling at heart, I must poke up my head from time to time to watch the widening shore and mark where the last shower of bullets had torn the waters.

Now we were close at hand, and every man rose on a knee, waiting the order to jump ashore. "I'm leaving you now, sir," came the lieutenant's high voice. "They'll land you from shore, sir!" The launch slowed up, cast us off and backed out to sea, and on we passed under our own way. "Hey, there," the lieutenant shouted, "get this barge ashore!" And that was the last I saw of the launch, for, if she were brave, she was prudent, and I heard her chug-chug for safer waters.

A party of men ran across the beach, caught our ropes and threw themselves with a will to hauling us ashore. The beach shelved slowly into the water, so that we scraped on the pebbles some way out. There was overmuch shrapnel for happiness, and though we had passed the warmest zone, it looked yet more restful across the beach. "That's as far as she'll come!" someone on the rope was calling out. "Lower the front board! The beach is hard enough: you must run the guns from where you are!"

Our fellows were already at the chains holding up the front of the barge, and now the board went down with a splash, and the gunners fell to rolling out the first gun. I jumped on to the side of the barge, and worked forward as fast as I might. The colonel and adjutant were scrambling ashore, and in the crowd there was a good chance of losing them. The sergeant-major stood in the water ordering the handling of the gun; and just then the gun ran into the water and into the sergeant-major too. Down he went on his back, and I thought that was the end of him. But there was no time for looking, the colonel had vanished into the crowd. Through the water I went, splashed on to the beach, and chased him over the shifting shingle. Not far off I caught him, talking to Colonel Irons, who was already on the scene. He was frowning and answering in an impatient way. I held him in the tail of my eye, and looked round. I was jumpy, for the beach was quite without cover; and who knew when a shell would burst at the proper angle and come tearing over in our direction?

Men moved about me with haste and purpose; and the loudest noise was the buzzing of the wireless plant, which spelt its messages at racing speed, nor stopped a moment.

Then my eye fell on the first dead man. He

lay on his back where the waves moved up and down across the sand, so that part of him was soaking wet and part quite dry. His fingers were stiff and spread out, and his flesh was a dirty patchy colour, and his mouth smiled a vacant smile. Yet doubtless somewhere at home a wife or mother prayed for his safekeeping. "So be it," said I, "so be it," and I looked another way.

There seemed no special regiments down here: men of all corps moved about, and officers were as frequent as privates. Nobody shot at anything, none flourished swords, there was not an enemy to be discovered. The place was more like the general room of a large bank or public office, where everyone is going somewhere, and nobody goes anywhere.

Already the army had left enduring marks. Two newly shovelled roads started off into the interior; a giant stack of provisions was growing a few yards from the waterline, and barges dumped quantities of small-arms ammunition on the sand. On the side of the hills many a man dug at his first funk-hole.

The anchorage was not a whit less busy than the beach. Infantry reinforcements came in steadily, ammunition barges and provision boats approached or lay at anchor close in shore. Pinnaces and rowing boats dodged round and round one another. I had forgotten to tell of something else—about a Red Cross flag, opening and closing in the busy breezes, lay many a line of stretchers with their mangled loads; and, while the orderlies were yet busy at the bandages, fresh cases arrived.

The talk of Irons and the colonel came quite suddenly to an end, and Jackson turned round and strode over in my direction. I could see he was annoyed. He made me no sign, but went past me towards our barge, and very soon we had run into the adjutant waiting there. "The guns must go back!" the colonel began abruptly, and that was about all I heard; but he and Yards talked on for half a minute or more maybe, he vigorous and impatient, like a man much put out, and Yards quiet as always, lifting his eyebrows and pursing his mouth now and again. Later on I was told we were then retreating fast, and Birdwood believed the position must be given up at night. This may be the truth or not: there were many liars on that beach. Presently Yards went off to the barge. "You may stay, Lake," the colonel said, and with that he started over the pebbles in the direction we had first taken.

In certain places there were quite as many sailors as soldiers, for the navy was in charge of the landing. These sailors were in khaki dress; and, although maybe they were a scratch lot, they knew their work well.

Beside a stock of ammunition were two little midshipmen or naval cadets, two bantam cocks, guarding it, no doubt. They were no age at all, so that they must have been at trouble to get there, but either was protected by a weighty revolver at belt. This way and that way they bobbed like sparrows on a twig, and every time a shell clapped overhead they eyed each other and giggled and dived for shelter. And next instant out they bobbed again. They were jolly little fellows. One day, if nothing happens, they shall tell mighty stories to a beaming family while filling up on plum cake.

Round about here wandered an elderly admiral in blue coat and white trousers. He was a tough customer, a sort of " one of the bulldog breed." He seemed able to abuse everybody, soldiers besides sailors. There was ever a heartier pull on a rope when his eye went searching that way.

I lacked time to notice much, for what with the crowd, the shingly beach, and my weight of equipment, I was hard put to it to keep the colonel in sight. He went over the beach in long strides, as if out of temper with the whole affair.

We came to a place where a deep ravine ran into the hills. In winter the bottom of the ravine was probably a watercourse, but spring found it quite dry. The banks, densely covered with scrub, were steep and came close together, especially as one progressed, so that there was shelter from the shrapnel here. The headquarters of several units had found this out and taken refuge.

We went along the gully, which kept a straight course and mounted all the way. We went by several natural dug-outs all occupied, and presently came on Divisional Artillery. All the fellows were there, crowding as close to the right bank as possible. Constantly the shrapnel clapped over our heads and swept into the bushes near by; but we were fairly secure, especially when sitting down. I don't know where the shells came from, but they were able to find the way.

Divisional Artillery had reserved two funk-holes, one just above the other. In a wet season the mountain torrent surged round here. The funk-holes had been improved with digging, and the officers had the top one, and we men the other. A colonel and adjutant of the Indian mountain batteries also shared the place. In a few moments my colonel left and went back to the beach; but he told me to stay where I was. The afternoon was getting on, and it had come over cloudy, and a drizzle of rain set in. The place at once turned very melancholy. The officers put on their coats and talked among themselves in a cheerless way, and one went to sleep. The fellows by me were no better off. They had come over in the morning and were full of rumours, but had no sure news to give. We had captured countless guns, we had driven the Turks across the Peninsula, the affair seemed about over. But one thing was certain—that all day endless wounded had arrived from the firing line.

I unrolled my coat and put it on. The drizzle continued, but came to nothing more, though shadows of late afternoon presently wandered along. The leaves grew heavy with moisture and started to drip on to the ground, and the dusty watercourse looked like turning to a treacherous camping-ground. For safety's sake we sat close against the bank, and the drip of the leaves had a tricky way of creeping under the collar of a coat.

We huddled together and spoke little, and I wished well the colonel would return and take me after him again. Then the drizzle cleared up, and the sun came out in a watery fashion, and we had a tea or supper of the little biscuits given as rations. Three days' provisions hung about me, but warning had been given they might be forced to last five, and I was chary of dipping deeply into the bag. Someone offered me the bottom of a can of tea, and I washed the crumbs away with it.

The guns at sea had shut their mouths; but there was an endless bubbling noise all about us, and not very far off either. It was the roll of musketry. The enemy never tired of shelling the beach, and time after time shells came tearing over our way. They would have found it difficult to touch us where we were. It was rifle bullets that kept us against the wall.

It was said the place was peopled with snipers, which was possible enough, for the close, crooked bushes might have concealed a battalion of them. One could find comfort knowing they were little better off than we, for if they were hid, also they could not see to shoot. Yet to look over this ocean of bushes with its lurking army left a sense of uneasiness.

The Indian colonel sat down on a rock, and a native orderly took off his boots, and gently and at much length massaged his feet. He appeared to have had a hard day of it, and his face was yellow and seamed, while he sipped a pot of tea. And then our colonel turned up and drank himself, and fell to talking earnestly with Irons. I tried to read their faces, but ended up as wise as I began.

"Lake," the colonel called out, and I went over gladly enough. The adjutant was getting ready to go away, and I was signed briefly to follow him. We picked our road down the water-course and, wherever it widened at all or a bit of extra shelter was offered by the banks, we came on groups of officers and men, and were forced to step with care. In one or two cases a slender meal progressed; but more often two or three men pored over a map, or talked in low tones, or sat back in a gloomy contemplation. We were not long gaining the open beach. After his fashion Yards had said not a word; but he paused just here and looked about him for a few moments, and next we turned to the left hand, hanging as near to the base of the hills as we could.

The sun was setting, and streams of angry yellow light filled the western part of the sky. It was day still, in fact hardly twilight; but very soon evening would be come. The battleships had given up the bombardment; but nowhere else was there sign of night or sleep. Countless craft were yet busy at sea, over which came forward an evening haze. And the beach was full of men.

We were on solid ground, as the pebbles scarcely reached to here: we passed our original landing-place, and went on until another ravine in the hills opened before us. Where now we stood the sappers had driven the beginnings of a road, and farther on they cut steps up another steep pinch. It happened the enemy shrapnel was coming over very briskly, but all of it burst rather higher up. We stood a little while as we had done at the last gully mouth. Yards looked up and down the hill as if comparing it with directions given him, and then we went up this gully and very soon were ascending a sharp rise. At the summit, which was no great distance, we went round a bit of a shoulder on the hill, and all at once were right on top of an A Battery gun in action. So a gun was ashore after all! We bent down—all cover was behind us—and went across to the gun in lively fashion, and sat down a little to one side of it. There was no cover for anybody, and the shrapnel arrived so fast and so near that I found myself pretty jumpy again, to speak the truth. Yet it would have needed a handsome cheque to buy my seat. We were in a sort of cup between two small hills, and Heaven knows what was our target! I sat while they fired the last four shells, which were put in in a lively manner. The climax of the sunset had arrived, all one portion of the sky was angry yellow and red, and the remainder full of sullen moving clouds, which made the evening cheerless and unwanted. Day had not gone yet; there remained enough light to see some distance with ease, so that one could pick out the faces of the gunners and mark all they did.

Either we had made ourselves unpopular and the enemy searched for us, or else the spot was naturally unhealthy, for the Turkish shrapnel came tearing over this way in the most unpleasant manner, and often three or four puffs of smoke sailed over us at one moment. The shells burst a trifle to our right against the fiery sunset; but those moments were none too certain. Major Felix stood by the trail in the easiest manner, altering the corrector, and then, as fast as I have told it, the last shot was fired, the men left off their work, and the major turned round. Almost at once the enemy ceased fire, and the sunset was left to fade and the darkness to come on undisturbed by us.

The major came over, and Yards got up. I heard a little of what was said, and gathered we had engaged an enemy gun, and Felix believed he had silenced it. They stayed talking for a little time. I forgot them in the business of watching the sky and the sea and the land dissolve into shadows, and hearkening to the fierce roll of musketry, now very near at hand. Then Yards came over my way and said something in passing in a low tone, and I rose and followed him down towards the beach.

It was quite dark in the first gully when we got back. The sky had clouded right over again so that very few stars showed, and the drizzle of rain had recommenced in drifts which passed and came. Our camp was cramped and rough and damp; but there was no doubt it was the safest spot anywhere about. The adjutant went on to the higher place, and sat down with the officers. Several men were turning in for the night, that is, lying down as they were with boots off, on a bed of a blanket and an overcoat. This left us more pressed for room than ever, as nobody was willing to leave the immediate shelter of the bank. Coming last, I had last place, which seemed nowhere at all in a first look round in the dark. But later I found a space a yard or two lower down the watercourse. It was a stony bed and rather exposed; but I picked out the worst stones and rolled as close under the bank as possible. They were shelling us again, but at uncertain intervals, and not much of their energy was directed this way. But the shells which came over here burst with a blinding red flash, as in a picture from a story book.

In spite of the musketry roll and shell fire, the night managed to retain something of solitude and stillness. I took my boots off, made the regulation bed of a blanket and overcoat, and huddled myself up in it. The night was not cold, and we were well screened from wind; but the depressing drizzle managed to find a way everywhere. On occasion a patch of stars stared down from overhead, but hid themselves very quickly, and I found myself looking for their coming and going in a dazed sort of way. I had done no heavy work, but I was glad enough to be lying down. I was sleepy in no time. Rifle bullets struck into the bank frequently, though none of them very low; but the bushes moved at intervals, whether from the wind or from gathering raindrops I do not know; but often I could have vowed to moving bodies there—be it sniper or imagination, it made one wake up and listen. Truly I have slept in more secure bedrooms than that one.

The weather was clearing somewhat, the stars stayed out longer, and larger patches of sky uncovered. Those were the last things I remembered.

CHAPTER X

IN THE FIRING LINE

THAT first night on land was a restless night and a never-ending one, though everybody was up by the first streak of dawn. I woke and slept, woke up and slept. Twice the rain pattered in my face, forcing me to cover my head, then the men guarding a pool of water somewhere at hand relieved guard, and trod on me in the process. The colonel went away once, giving me his glasses and map case and other things to look after. Yet again I was wakened by two fellows close beside me. I came out of a doze, and heard them speaking in mysterious tones.

"There's a bloke moving in the bushes. I heard him sure. Is anybody round the other side?"

"I don't think so."

"It may be a sniper." The other fellow grunted. "We had better make certain." The other fellow grunted again. Something more was said, and one got up, went a little way into the bushes and poked about a bit with stick or bayonet, I could not see which. The search was without result, and he came back and lay down, and the conversation went on a while in whispers. I was dozing again when a couple of bullets plumped into the bank three or four foot overhead, and tiny showers of dirt trickled down. That woke me up with a vengeance. The night was much clearer, but damp and forbidding; and my circulation played tricks, for I seemed more exposed than I had believed. I moved my head about to find where to go, and in the end dragged everything a few yards lower down, where I was alone and could be closer in to our right bank. I felt more secure; but I was wide awake, and stayed so a long while. I doubt not all were glad when dawn arrived.

I got up feeling like a cat rubbed the wrong way. My clothes had not been off. Yet there was no wash nearer than the sea. In the manner of last night we had breakfast of biscuits and bully beef, sent down with a mouthful of water, and afterwards I sat huddled and yawning, picking my teeth with a twig from the nearest bush. It was pretty cold just then, and I wished the colonel would make a start on his travels. He was not long about it. Breakfast over and the world properly alight, we set off, turning as usual for the beach.

The beach was like yesterday, as crowded and as busy. There was more ammunition about, and a higher stack of provisions. Our battleships were moving, for action later on it might be, and Turkish shrapnel came over in merry morning bursts. We spent much time on the beach, and the sun rose high up at last. We went this way and that way and every way, tramping over the shingle and threading through the crowds. The colonel was full of business. He met endless officers, talked plans with some, and gave a how-de-do to others just ashore. Also there were long intervals of waiting, when one might look round and find out what was happening.

The morning was bright with sunshine, the air a trifle sharp. Over all the ocean mounted thin smoke lines from the battleships and transports. High up into the sky they went, for there was no wind to speak of. Between those waiting giants and the shore hurried the thousand small craft which already I have told you of. It was like grown-ups and children on an autumn morning, the elders rheumy and contained, the youngsters racing in good spirit.

Wandering thus, we came on a party of sailors leaning back on a rope lashed to a barge, I think. The group was large, and a warrant officer with a gold band on his sleeve took charge. The men were elderly or over youthful, naval reservists and recruits, said I, and I saw such pimply, ill-bred faces as London breeds. The warrant officer was short and vast of girth, and a khaki solar hat covered a face seamed and fiery from tropic suns and strong spirits. I thought of a barrel on legs. I warrant his wife made small demur when he packed up for the wars. He marched solemnly up and down the line of men, eyeing this one and that one, and giving short, sharp commands. The front men splashed in the water, and the tail of the line trailed across the beach; and all the while the shrapnel came over in a dirty fashion, clawing at the water sometimes, and sometimes spurting on to the pebbles. I could not help measuring the distance to the friendly cliffs; but ill it became one to consider retreat, and I swelled my chest and looked as though I liked it.

Now the men on the rope pulled away, some with an even pull and some in a heartless, jerky fashion, for their minds were on the shells hurling over. There were those who dropped down nearly to the ground, and grinned in sheepish and unhappy manner. The warrant officer trod heavily up and down as cool as you like, and I wondered how soon he would say something—something to the point, I mean. All suddenly sounded a rush and a bang right over our heads, and that poor line of cockneys crouched this way and that, and a fellow dropped the rope and ran away under the cliff. The warrant officer turned round—revolved is the word, for round objects revolve—and he did not wave his arms or do any other thing, lest he should burst perhaps; but he roared out—and I liked his voice less than the shrapnel—"Come out of that, you skulker! If you be killed, you be killed!" Feebly the man came back, and the rope straightened again, and the barge came ashore.

"My salute, sir. In all humility Gunner Lake offers his salute."

Finally the colonel's business on the beach ended, and he went the way I had gone overnight.

The sappers had driven the road out of sight, and farther on the stairway over the hill was completed. We followed up the ravine, until I made sure we were about to look for the A Battery gun; but we moved somewhat to the right hand and gained the crest that way. I say "gained the crest," but we stopped just short of the top, for on the farther side went forward with utmost spirit a dainty little battle. Had all been quiet one would have looked and beheld only the wilderness, for the guns were hidden in odd clumps of scrub, and of infantry there was no sign. Later I found a few of them in a trench behind the guns and quite close to us. I wondered then what they did there.

Now the sun had climbed up into the sky, a jolly warming sun who searched alike open and thicket with his glances. To be sure, he drew away to him the fresh morning scents; but he left all the scrubland silvery and quivering, and threw a glad haze over the open country. Hills and valleys were about us, and next a broad plain, and beyond that the great breast of Achi-Baba. Hills and valleys were before us, and the flat sea behind.

We stayed but a few instants just here ere a bullet skimmed by and set us thinking of healthier places. It happened that on the right of this crest was a scooped-out spot, not exactly a trench, probably some old Turkish observing station. The colonel saw there what he wanted, and we went for it at the double, jumped down into it and dropped on our knees. It had a depth of three or four foot, and we could stay fairly protected and look over the top and scan the whole countryside. The morning was wonderfully pretty —the place was ablaze with sunlights, browns and smoky blues. When one found the guns and gunners, which was only possible of those near by, their dress harmonised so exactly that they did not offend. And the roar of battle was less hideous here. The musketry rolled from all around, and the hissing bursts of machine guns were born and died. There was the plucky "bang-bang" of a mountain battery, and the heavier voice of our own gun, which opened its mouth ever and anon. But there was nothing of that bellow of the ponderous guns at sea.

I was on my knees with only my head above the parapet, and not an inch more of that than need be. The firing came from all over the place, so much so that one was put to it to tell which was from us and which from the enemy. Thus an extra inch was of account.

Briskly as went forward the battle, it must wait my attention while I roamed a farmer's eye across the landscape. All was so charming and so full of contrast. We—the colonel and I—were perched in a land of heights and depths, which in happier days may have grazed lean flocks of sheep and goats. Over in the distance there was a wide flat country of vines and cropland, even now filling with the harvest. Humble homes were hid there, with anxious wife or aged mother as guardian. For the lords had gone forth, changing the sickle for the musket.

Somewhere in that flat country the enemy lay, though I never picked them up, as I was without glasses. I found our men slowly, and in every case suddenly. They were beneath us, and rather to the left hand. A mountain gun and our own A Battery gun were close—quite close, a matter of yards. Yet one must look keenly to see the brown puggareed men at their posts, and our own green-uniformed gunners beyond. It was their movements and the flashes which made this possible.

I have said there was an old trench behind the guns, filled with a number of our infantry. It had little depth, and from up here one might look right in. The fellows crouched or sat, rifle in hand, helping nothing towards the business. I could not understand it.

Now a track ran round the shoulder of our hill, joining the beach with a broad valley thrusting into the mountains. One could not follow the course of the valley far, as hills interrupted; but I had the belief that at its head lay the trenches our infantry held. The track I speak of curved in front of the guns, and was exposed all the way to such attentions as the enemy liked to give. Yet continually passengers passed up and down. All manner of men went, and all paces they went at. There were curious, lonely infantrymen, who came out of the valley and disappeared towards the beach. There were those who passed at a walk, and those who went by at a halting run, dodging before the guns and losing themselves in no time. Several lines of stretcher cases arrived at slower pace, or a single stretcher advanced down the road, or even a walking wounded man appeared, leaning on the shoulder of a friend. Not one who went that way but was dusty, parched, and tired. And some men would return towards the valley—stretcher-bearers in general case. Some ran over the open as fast as weariness allowed, but others plodded forward worn past anxiety.

But of all who came and went, I remembered best two men approaching with utmost slowness from the valley. They were a chaplain and a wounded man whom he supported. I watched them all the way, for they came so slowly and with such small concern of the hubbub round; the chaplain engrossed in his task, and the wounded man beyond all caring for what befell. They passed near to us, at one time below our breastwork, the chaplain talking to his friend or looking along the path towards the hospitals on the beach. I am glad to have seen those men go by.

Merrily the fight went forward. Officers came up beside us, and talked a little with the colonel and watched a little, and went away again. One who came was Major Andrews, and I heard we were landing more guns, and some of the Staff were on the way over. He spoke of meeting them and went off.

All the while the colonel said never a word to me; but he scanned the field with his glasses, and once or twice he used a telescope. Often he would look towards the beach and curse the absence of his guns.

This cup in the hills was not the only spot of battle: the enemy still remembered the beach and the sea, and many a shell went whistling past us over that way. I began to tire of the place, and would have welcomed a move; but just then I caught sight of some of our Staff climbing from the beach. They had just landed, for they were loaded with flags and field telephones, besides personal equipment. They panted from their efforts, and coming to the top of the rise nearly below us, bunched together in the open, and looked as though they knew it too. I was sending a good-day nod from my funk-hole, when the colonel brushed me on one side, and, lifting over the parapet all of his head that was wanted, called out impatiently to Mr. Gardiner in charge.

"What about the guns, Mr. Gardiner? What have you done with them?"

"They're here, sir. We met the major!"

And then there followed explanations, and it turned out the guns were going the wrong way, and Gardiner went back in a hurry, put about for the first time.

Though things straightened finally, the morning was confused and full of running about. Afternoon was no better. Until evening I followed on the colonel's heels; and he went this way, that way, and every way, over the shingle, and up and down the small hills which met the beach. All day the shells came from inland, tumbling about us at every angle, or tearing up the waters for a brief moment. All day the transports sent reinforcements; and new guns and barges of ammunition and provisions arrived. The hospital ships sailed away, and others steamed from the horizon. Men dug in wherever an inch of cover was. Gangs of sappers drove roads, and toiling lines of men dragged the field guns from the beach along the roads to positions on the hills. Every hour left us surer of our footing.

By night we artillery fellows—those who had got over—had made our headquarters near by the little battlefield of the morning. When the colonel and I came back, men were digging in the guns.

It was necessary to keep communication through the night with Divisional Artillery by means of lamp signals. The Staff were taking turns at this. My turn was somewhere about the middle of the night, so I dug a shallow funk-hole, and when the stars came out took off my boots and lay down. The bad weather had long cleared away, and the stars were very bright.

"So another day was ending, and again came darkness to cover up the ruin and the agony. Higher were heaped the dead, and braver were the ranks of the maimed. More men had stood their trial, had proven themselves or had been found wanting. And you, Gunner Lake, have you thanked the God of Battle that you have stayed unafraid?"

Old Grandmother Lake used to take me, a small boy, to her knee, and bid me pray for the welfare of the British army. Now her grandsons fight in many corners of the world. Among the battle maidens Grandmother Lake sits in Valhalla and waits serenely their coming.

Hardly was I asleep when someone shook me by the shoulder. I opened my eyes to find the stars shining, and Wilkinson kneeling beside me.

"What's the time?" I mumbled.

"Twelve o'clock and your shift." I muttered, yawned, and sat up.

"What's to be done?"

"Watch Divisional Artillery for any lamp signals. Do an hour and wake Foster. He's next man."

I nodded, and while I let out another yawn Wilkinson disappeared. With many an unuttered curse I got to my feet. I found a weary wind had risen, as full of toothache as a stick of nougat. I put my coat on, turning up the collar; and over head and neck I pulled a big woollen cap, thanking as I did so the good women of Melbourne that had knitted it. I stumbled along the track to a better spot and sat down. The stars shone clearly; but the sea, the hillsides, and even more so the beach were folded in gloom. Like the boiling of a pot sounded ceaseless distant musketry fire—low now and fitful; now waking to life—never, never silent. Every few minutes a shell came whistling overhead, to burst threateningly in the sea. The transports had drawn several miles away, the battleships lay before them; and in and out moved restless destroyers. Other craft were there—numberless they seemed and of every kind—anchored among the shadows closer in shore. I saw the Morse lamps winking to one another, and felt companionship, knowing others watched with me. I followed great yellow search-lights in ceaseless journeyings round the bay, and knew that others too guarded the sleeping multitude.

Soon I stood up. The wind stirred perpetually the low bushes; but I heard few sounds of it. My mind was weary with the day just over: I saw anew dead men, torn beasts: and heard the voices of guns, and the thousand echoes of battle. Useless sacrifice the struggle seemed at this solemn hour. Presently the night air crept through my coat, and sent my hands into pockets and myself moving up and down. For all my watching no signal appeared; but instead my footsteps sounded ever more mournfully on the path. Nobody was here to say an army slept in the ragged scrub on either side. Finally, to lose my thoughts, I fell to putting together a battle prayer.

EVENING BATTLE PRAYER

Trench by trench, along the line,
  Dies the spluttering musketry;
And the gunners at their guns
  Lay the heavy shrapnel by.
Now the wearied flying-man
  Glides in circles from the sky:
And, across the dimming bay,
Move the armoured ships away.
God of Battle! God of Right!
Guard and guide Thy troops this night!

Here and here, among the hills,
  Gleam the tiny supper fires;
There and there a hard-spent man
  To a barren bed retires.

Now across the darkened bowl,
Pass the stars on their patrol,
Staring down on War's still feast,
Mangled man and broken beast.
God of Battle! God of Right!
Guard and guide Thy troops this night!

Steps and voices were coming behind me. Instantly I woke up and drew into deeper shadow, and stood there several moments while the shuffling sounds came forward. They proved to be a stretcher party, arriving painfully round the bend in the path.

There was a difficult place, where the ground sloped abruptly; but with much tenderness the Red Cross men lifted their burdens past. I left the path altogether for them to file by, and they did so—a sorrowful, halting procession—one lying here with torn shoulder, one here with a vast bloody wrap about his face, one here with shattered feet—so they went by silent and still, with closed eyes and grey faces.

After them shambled a numerous crowd with bandaged arms, and legs bound up, talking in low tones and smoking cigarettes. I heard a thin voice say, "Don't think much of these smokes; but a bloke'll take on anything here." After followed a gruff voice. "Blarsted bad luck getting put out second day. Corporal Davis got outed altogether: you know 'im, a big bouncing brute in D Company. 'E got a bullet through the heart, and jumped about ten foot in the air." And then a third voice. "I got three in the arm from a swine of a machine gun. Aching like Hell!" So from the trenches they came, and passed to the Red Cross station on the beach.

My hour was up, the watch over; gladly I hurried off and pulled my relief out of bed. Next minute the blankets were over me, and I was falling asleep.

CHAPTER XI

ACTION FRONT

FAINTEST dawn climbed over the bay as I woke up in the morning. I opened one eye and then the other, and took courage and propped myself on an elbow. It was nearly dark; but already the beach showed life and movement, and vague battleships were taking up new stations out at sea. Nobody near by seemed awake, the bushes looked empty and rather mysterious; but far off the everlasting musketry went on—dying, growing, and dying away again. I took a long look round until courage failed me, when back I went under the blanket.

From that bed cut in the hillside, I watched the morning growing out of night. Again—and still again—new sights, new sounds were born. The curves among the hills took shape; the waters moved into life; and from a grey distance rose the faint peaks of Imbros. The bay filled with vessels—small and great. Cruisers and churlish battleships manœuvred from point to point; and scouts and destroyers sped along a thoroughfare where mine-sweepers, trawlers, tugboats, colliers, barges, pontoons, lifeboats, and rowing-boats jostled one another all the way. The transports rode beyond this highway, with thin smoke lines creeping to the sky; and with them waited the hospital ships for the burden the day would bring. While yet I watched, morning fully broke. I threw aside the blanket, and sat up; and put out a hand for my boots.

The beach quickly resembled the market-place of a town. Men in groups or singly hurried this way and that—Red Cross men bore wounded on stretchers, Indians led mules, sailors in parties hauled ashore guns and their waggons, artillerymen loaded themselves with ammunition, infantrymen formed up for a return to the trenches, Greeks stabled donkeys, Army Service men stacked high piles of bully beef and tins of biscuit. Guns and limbers blocked the way, lines of wounded lay beneath the shelter of the cliffs, farther on were ingathering vast stores of provisions, and farther yet tanks for fresh water stood where the waves lapped the pebbles.

Sacks of flour were thrown into growing heaps, and beside them sacks of sugar. Cases of tea were dumped upon the sand. Cheeses were arriving, and sides of bacon. Sheets of tin roofing lay on one another, waiting for the shins of the unwary.

Men loaded lengths of wood for bomb-proof roofings and men staggered under bales of hay. Gangs of sappers drove roads along the hillsides, and telephonists ran wires from bush to bush. Infantry parties bore sandbags on their heads towards the firing line, and other parties trudged uphill, loaded with water-bottles. Men mooched round with rifles on their backs, and men were there with picks and shovels. The murmurs of life rose up like a mighty ocean tide.

The hillside, too, awoke: it became peopled with men drawing on shirts and pulling at boots. Blue blankets appeared on half the bushes, waiting for the tardy sun; later wisps of smoke curled up from fifty places. Already our gunners were lingering round their guns, placing last sandbags along the parapets, and stacking the ammunition brought by men toiling up the hill. I was surprised at all that had gone forward while I slept. The guns were lowered nearly to the ground level, and protected by heavy ramparts of earth and sandbags, masked with leafy boughs. Trenches for approach ran out, and telephone wires linked up the observing station. The funk-holes for the gunners ran beside the guns.

Now at last, if reluctantly, the sun got up. I could not see him, but his beams came creeping round the corner. They made the bushland warm and cheerful, and the damp fled away from the patches of brown earth which appeared in places on the hills. The insects came out from cracks and crevices, and set briskly on new travels; and the little birds which were lovemaking in the greenery puffed their breasts out, and chirruped with morning confidence. It was going to be a tropic day.

The cook, however he was, had boiled some tea and fried rashers of bacon. He sent me a " Cooee," and I went over with a mess tin. There were half a dozen about the fire holding out pannikins for filling; and Hawkins was crouched among the ashes, stirring an evil-looking mess meant for Welsh rabbit. He was too interested to look up; but the others greeted me with "Well, and how are things?" I did not feel talkative myself, and answered by an all-round nod.

There were two rashers of bacon each, and as many biscuits as a man wanted. I went back to my funk-hole, balancing the biscuits and bacon in one hand and a pot of tea in the other.

Just then the old balloon went up.

I had grown so used to the perpetual musketry fire that I no longer heard it; and though the enemy still shelled us in a casual manner, they were overshooting the mark, and most of their endeavours ended in the sea. Sometimes, with a whizz and a bang, a hail of bullets descended on the beach, and some poor fellow would fall down, and maybe two or three others hobble away; but this was very seldom. From where we sat eating on the hillside we received no more notice than the tunes of shells in their passage, the hum of strayed bullets, and the sounds of an angry beehive when a machine gun sent part of a charge through space.

But just now one of the battleships drew to a standstill and swung slowly about; and even while I poured the pannikin of tea in joyous stream down my throat, with a roar like the last trump she vomited a thousand-pound shell half-across the peninsula. As I stopped choking, a cruiser took up the running; and behold another round in the battle had begun.

I hurried breakfast after this, and hung within call of the observing station. The other fellows too seemed to think our ball would soon open, for they stretched jaws wide on the biscuits and bacon, and that duty done, collected the flags and telephones. The usual abuse was exchanged when nothing could be found.

"What the hell have you done with those flags? Can't you leave a blasted cove's things alone for a minute? They were there before breakfast!"

"I've not touched your damned things. You want a nurse, you do!"

The colonel, the adjutant, the sergeant-major, and Wilkinson, as telephonist, climbed presently up to the brigade observing station. Not far away, and lower down, Major Felix, his sergeant-major, and telephonist took possession of a dug-out—the B Battery observing station was higher up, to the left hand. The whole position was congested, but where was the room? A dozen yards below the brigade observing station Eaves curled himself up, his head fastened to a telephone running to Divisional Artillery; and I received orders to perch myself half-way between him and the observing station, under the shelter of an overhanging ledge.

The bombardment grew in volume: battleship after battleship engaged a target. Like a colossal thunderstorm the explosions roared around the bay. The very ground was a-tremble. Now the veteran *Triumph* opened fire; and the *Queen Elizabeth* drew farther out and came to a standstill. I became aware that the sun was mounting and his beams had turned unpleasantly fierce. There was not a puff of wind, there was not a cloud in the sky; and the blue waters of Saros were without ruffle or furrow. I became aware that the musketry was more intense, and that machine guns were opening in sharp bursts along the lines. We for our part were ready now—the gunners waiting in the funk-hole behind the guns, the section commanders at their posts, Major Felix megaphone in hand. But still no order for us came through.

The effect of the ships' fire quickly became apparent, insomuch as the enemy woke up with a vengeance, and answered with salvos of shrapnel and lyddite, following hard on one another's heels, and coming over our heads with a rush and a bang which were unholy, to say the least.

Many of the salvos fell about the craft in the bay, but some were better timed, and poured into the bushes, sending us close into whatever shelter was handy, or hissed on to the crowded beach, where there was a sporting chance of bagging anything from generals to tin cans. May be after a lucky shot a riot would start among the mules, or some poor chap would go to his Maker or fall down winged: and then would go forward a cry for stretcher-bearers and Red Cross men. Or may be a party hauling at some gun would scatter without warning behind a pile of stores, like mice into a hole. Yet in that bustling thoroughfare it was strange how few were the accidents.

Long ago conversation had grown impossible; but there would be moments of silence when from the head of the valley descended very plainly the frantic splutter of musketry, the fierce bursts of machine guns, and the game barking of our little Indian mountain batteries. Also at such times there rose up many strange cries from the beach. Then I could hear distinctly the loud buzz of the wireless plant calling to the navy what targets to engage. By now we gunners were all close in our funk-holes; but the road from the valley was still populous with long processions of wounded toiling to the Red Cross headquarters below.

An infantry fellow in fighting order and with a haversack on his back came scrambling up the hill just then, found room beside me and planted himself there. He could not speak for panting and was ready to break down; but the place he secured was fairly well protected, and confidence came back with breath. I glanced over him as he crouched there: he was a thin, weakly-bred fellow, and plainly a liar. I said nothing to him because he was upset, and because the sun was getting too hot for talking; but I went on watching the beach very hard.

"Halloa, cobber," he said at last.

"Hallo," I answered, and turned towards him.

He looked at me out of palest blue eyes. "I

just come from the firing line," he said. "It's murder there. What are you blokes doing?"

"Going to shoot soon, I suppose," said I.

"You ought ter be up in the firin' line. They could do with you."

"Oh!" I answered.

"Gettin' any losses here?"

"Most of the fire is going over, but we'll be shooting in a minute or two, and that ought to open the ball in earnest."

He said nothing to this; but soon, very soon, he was up and creeping away. He passed from view, but not towards the firing line.

Yes, it was going to be a hot day. I pushed my finger into the neck of my shirt, which already was clammy with perspiration. A haze had fallen over the more distant parts of the bay; and round my ears a solitary fly buzzed with persistence worthy of a nobler cause. Neither shrapnel nor lyddite could move him. Yes, it was going to be a hot day!

Orders were through. Just near me someone called out: it was Major Felix, a megaphone to his mouth. He shouted something, and I caught most of it.

"Infantry advancing! Aiming point, left ridge of Battleship Hill! Line of fire, twenty degrees three-ough minutes right. Corrector one-five-ough ——three-six hundred! Angle of sight three degrees one-ough minutes elevation! One round battery fire!"

The section commander saluted, and cried to his sergeants, the sergeants, kneeling at the trails, saluted and turned to the gunners. No. 3, on the left seat, laid the gun; No. 6 set the fuse, and No. 5 passed the shell to No. 4. No. 2, on the right-hand seat, opened the breech, No. 4 pushed home the shell, No. 2 closed the breech again. Then came a pause, then "Fire" was given, though I could not hear it. But there followed a mighty uproar, which seemed to beat the ground and plunge back again on to my ears, the boughs about the guns sprang into the air, long tongues of flame leaped forth, and the gun-barrels slid backwards and into place again.

The seconds went by. Again Major Felix was shouting. "C gun five minutes more left! Shorten corrector six! Drop two-ough-ough! Repeat!"

"What?" the section commander shouted.

"C Gun Five Minutes More Left! Shorten Corrector Six! Drop Two-ough-ough! Repeat!"

"What?" the section commander shouted.

"C GUN FIVE MINUTES MORE LEFT! SHORTEN CORRECTOR SIX! DROP TWO-OUGH-OUGH! REPEAT!"

The section commander saluted and turned to his sergeants, the sergeants saluted and directed the gunners, and again the yellow flames stabbed the air, and the uproar seemed to rebound and strike me.

A third time the order came: "C gun two minutes more left! Drop five-ough! Gunfire!"

We were into it with a vengeance now: by land, by sea equally engaged. Never a moment slackened the enemy fire: rather the sky became more terrible with the voices of travelling shells, and more beautiful with delicate bursts of shrapnel. At intervals mighty howitzer shells rumbled solemnly through space, and plunged into the sea amid columns of spray. We gunners must soon have made ourselves unwelcome, for the enemy guns started to search for us, and quickly the game of hide and seek became too hot for pleasure. I was still perched under the projecting ledge; but my time was coming. Eaves lifted up his transmitter and began to call—" 'Ullo 'Ullo!" A message was coming through from Divisional Artillery. Presently, receiver at ear, Eaves wrote it heavily down. Next he read it slowly through. He was quite undisturbed: he was a good man, was Eaves. Then he beckoned me. " 'Ere you are," he said, holding out the message in a hairy hand.

I took the paper and began to crawl up the bank to the observing station. Matters were livelier than ever in the open. Shells were bursting like the devils of hell, and rifle bullets went by with the slashing sound of steel drawn tightly on steel. The ascent was a matter of seconds, and I leaned over the edge of the dug-out. Wilkinson, telephone at ear, lay in a half-moon in a funk-hole of his own; and in the main funk-hole sat the colonel, adjutant, and sergeant-major with maps across their knees. An argument was going on. News was through we were shelling our own infantry. "They're dirty liars!" I heard the colonel burst out—and then the message was taken in, and I was beckoned away by a quick gesture.

Round I went again, and down the hill. The major was shouting once more.

"Aiming point, straight edge of Gaba Tepeh! Two degrees four-five minutes elevation! Corrector one-four-five-three-four hundred! One round battery fire!"

The guns roared out, the long flames stabbed the air. A call came—"One gun out of action, sir." "What's wrong?" "What?" "What's wrong?" "Finding out!" "All guns seven degrees more left. Shorten corrector six! Drop one-fifty! Gunfire!"

I had kept small account of the time, for I discovered next that the morning was growing old. I had no watch; but the sun had moved well across to our right hand, and the last patches of shade were disappearing. I blew into the hot air, and pushed a hand across my forehead. Still the cannonade went on, still the earth trembled, still the voice behind called out new orders. "Last target was F. Next target will be registered as H" fell on my dazed ears.

Then I noticed an aeroplane coming up from the south over the Turkish lines. Tender puffs of shrapnel followed its course. A second one sailed far to the left, a dot in a hazy distance. The man in the balloon still watched away, well out of reach of the longest gun. Presently the aeroplanes faded from sight, and I went back to the old pastime of staring at the beach.

Heat and howitzers, shrapnel and sunstroke,

alike could not affect the buzzing throng there. From my perch I looked down on to another world. Directly below lay the Red Cross jetty whence pinnaces towed long strings of boats to the hospital ships. A white flag with a red cross waved at the jetty end. The boats lay into the sides, and the wounded men were borne along the planking, and placed in rows upon the decks. Unhappily, the spot was searched by enemy fire, and more than one poor fellow, who had survived long suffering, met his end lying there while the boats filled up. The wharf was in charge of a naval party, with a short-tempered old brute in blue jacket and white trousers in command. He stood in the middle of the thoroughfare, indifferent to everything, and bellowed through a megaphone at the Red Cross men. I thought if anything happened to him there, Old Nick would have a rough time down below. Whenever the firing lulled, up came his voice.

"I am taking severe stretcher cases only. Forward some severe stretcher cases. Yes, sir, I said stretcher cases only. My God, sir, are you the fool or am I?" And he added something else I won't put down. Then would come another lull. "Now I shall take some standing-up cases."

As fast as the pinnaces and their loads steamed to sea, new boats put into harbour; and throughout the day the procession of stretchers moving to the wharf did not stop. As the boats filled with recumbent men, all odd spaces were taken by those who still could stand or sit erect; and these clambered painfully aboard with staring bandages round head or arm. Weary and broken were the most, I grant; yet more than once that day a voice piped out: "Are we downhearted?" and a chorus answered "No!" With shrapnel flecking the waters, and too often bursting overhead, string after string of loaded boats turned to the mother ship; and with their departure the bellow ever came up again, "I am taking severe stretcher cases! Forward me some stretcher cases!"

"C gun two minutes more right! Drop five-ough! Repeat!" The battle was wearing on. I wondered how we did on the right, and if the New Zealanders held firmly to the left.

Eaves beckoned violently: a message had arrived from Divisional Artillery. I went across and watched him put it laboriously to paper. "Guns in action, three o'clock five degrees east of Battleship Hill. Engage them." I jerked the form from him, and started again for the observing station.

There was fascination as well as risk in the scramble through the open, where Death roamed overhead with threatening voice. I reached the big dug-out, leaned over, tossed in the message, and met the abrupt signal to return. Down I went, slipping and springing from tuft to tuft, and falling on my back somewhere near the ledge. Just here a brain wave came along: I bethought me of a four days' beard, and rising up, bolted on to my own funk-hole at the bottom of the hill. Into my kit I dived, caught up the shaving tackle, and was back again at the ledge while you could count fifty. There I lay and perspired, while the voice of Major Felix called out the new target.

"Guns in action! Aiming point right-hand edge of Battleship Hill! Line of fire five degrees five minutes right! Corrector one-five-ough—three-three hundred! Angle of sight three degrees three-five minutes elevation! One round battery fire!"

I fell to watching the bay again. The transports lay at anchor beyond range of enemy guns, and the battleships riding at their stations never ceased to send loud voices over the deep. But nearer shore a thousand craft sped to and fro. Now and now again, a monster shell rumbled out of the hills, and rent a chasm in the even sea; but still the craft came and went, nor turned their course a hair's breadth. Truly luck followed us this day.

But while I watched a hideous burst of smoke and coal dust leaped from a mine-sweeper, and all at once she fell a-shivering. Smoke and dust drifted away, and I scanned her keenly, but could make out no harm.

Just now the good *Queen Bess* picked up a target—a howitzer in action on a far crest. I saw her swing at her station: I saw her move out to sea.

He was no fool, that howitzer. He crouched behind his sandbag ramparts, and boomed defiance at the foul infidel guns. Upon his stout overhead cover shells and shrapnel burst in vain.

But he had not met the good *Queen Bess.*

The good *Queen Bess* moved out to sea, and there the good *Queen Bess* lay to: with care she read her angles, with cunning she laid her guns. She watched, she quivered—and with a bellow of rage she hurled a two-thousand-pound shell. She missed the howitzer and struck the crest below; and away went the crest, and away went the howitzer.

Somewhere else, drawn by ten horses, an enemy field gun trotted into the open. There he unlimbered, and the team turned for cover. But in the bay a British boat was watching, and forth leaped two flames. There was a whirlwind where the gun had been. The whirlwind climbed towards the sky. But there was no gun; there were no horses; there were no men. And many souls were speeding up to Allah.

And—thus runs the legend—where the fight raged thickest this day, the good *Queen Bess* emptied a round from a fifteen-inch gun, whose shrapnel spreads a mile, and wiped from earth two companies of infantry. "Allah! Allah! Thy courtyards will be filled this night!"

"All guns three degrees more right! Shorten corrector six! Drop one-five-ough! Repeat!"

I began to consider my shaving. Every trace of shade had gone—as far as I was concerned, that is to say. I sat leaning forward on a bare ledge, and the sun. blazed in my face. "So be it," I muttered and swore, and spread out the shaving tackle. Into a pannikin went a few drops of water, meaning a drink lost; and picking up the soap from the sand, I rubbed it over my face. I was hot, tired, thirsty, and sticky with perspiration. A fur had grown over the roof of my mouth, for I was unwashed, and my clothes had not been off for half a week. And I thought—"Damn this! Is this life for the next two years, with maybe a bullet as final bonus? Damn this!" said I.

I looked down on the highway of the beach, where lines of wounded moved towards the boats; where under the cliffs doctors probed red wounds, and carved at arms and legs; where Indians urged mules; where sailors toiled at guns and waggons, and midget midshipmen or naval cadets, or whatever they were, ran round with mighty revolvers strapped at their hips; where the wireless man sent out his buzz—buzz—buzz; where cursing Army Service men hauled in new barges of provisions; where Greeks screamed at donkeys, and kept a wide eye on shelter; where sappers wielded picks; where officers of many ranks dodged from point to point, and waved hands and flourished canes; where men pumped water into tanks from barges. And I looked out at sea where the battleships rocked out flame; where destroyers sped up and down; where men toiled at oars; where boats emptied reinforcements on to shore; where pinnaces hooted; where loaded barges swung at anchor. I looked and I said: "Gunner Lake, not yet is the hour for complaint."

Eaves woke me up. He waved a message form.

I took it without a word, and started up to the observing station. The soap was on my face, and was a crust by the time I was back again. However, I made a second start at shaving when I found breath. To be honest, I was shy of the business. The ground shivered continually under the cannonade, and I pictured a hand slipping and a gallant gunner going to his doom. At last, with tender care, I engaged an upper jaw. I left a nick about half-way down, and three others at the point of the chin, and from there passed in a passage of blood to the farther side. It cost me many an oath, but the victory was mine.

I was putting things away with lighter heart, when my eye fell on the trawler I had seen shelled: she was going down by the stern. Already the water lapped her gunwales, and crept on to the deck. I watched entranced.

She was sinking very slowly—so slowly that the minutes made no difference—still when I looked away and looked again, the ocean had crept higher up her sides. It was a noble end for an ancient fishing tub. At intervals high-bursting shrapnel raked her from bows to stern; and the guns kept up a thunder that would follow her below the waves. And as I watched—ye gods!—the crew put off in an open boat, and pulled with the heart of a Yarra eight through a sea knocked up with bullets. Methought in days to come, in some village pothouse—when the mellow ale had done its work—methought of certain hoary seamen who would swell their chests and relate to youth agape the epic of stout times departed.

Up I scrambled with another message, and down I came again. Major Felix and his section commander were shouting to one another.

"We can't clear the crest at two-four hundred!"

"What?"

"The crest at two-four hundred!"

Streams of wounded still flowed along the road from the valley head. One Red Cross fellow with a donkey had passed twice or thrice that day. He was becoming known to all: they said no fire disturbed him. On his donkey he would mount a man wounded in leg or foot. He was always cheerful and never tired.

Now a mule battery laden with guns and ammunition wound like a serpent up the narrow way. I marked it twisting up and up the ridge, until the crest came between, and only a dead mule stayed to tell of the passage.

Eaves was beckoning again. I leaned forward and caught the message. Up through the tufty grasses I went, and then down again to my ledge. Next moment I was climbing the hill once more.

"All guns ten minutes more right! Shorten corrector four. Drop five-ough; battery fire!"

I was very weary of the uproar, and I looked over to the Red Cross jetty. A group of sailors waited on the quay while a string of boats drew in. I saw them break and scatter; I saw the puff of a bursting shell; and down went one poor fellow, and away into cover staggered another. A couple of comrades ran back and picked up the fallen man, and the group passed under the cliff, where I could not follow.

"Stop!" Major Felix was shouting. "Stop!" There was the roar of the firing gun. "Who fired then?" There were quick answers and quick replies. The major burst out: "Take that sergeant off that gun, and put him under arrest!" There were more answers and replies. "All right," the major shouted again. "Let him carry on; I shall see him after!" Again his voice came to me. "Guns in action at C. Aiming point left edge of false ridge. Line of fire five degrees one-five minutes right! Corrector one-five-ough—three-nine hundred! Angle of sight three degrees one-ough minutes elevation. One round battery fire!"

Messages began to hurry through, and I was tired out with climbing up and down. Finally, when there was time to sit still, I found an infantry fellow perched on my ledge. He looked hot and fagged.

"This dirty sun settles a cove quick," he said. And he said no more. I crouched beside him.

"How are things going? Have you heard?" I said.

"Bonza! We've got 'em on the move. They say the British are joining us at five o'clock to-night. We've been cut up a good bit; but the navy has sent thousands of the other blokes skyhigh. I was sent here with a wounded man, and must get back. I'll make a start. Well, so long, mate."

"So long," I answered.

He watched for the sky to clear of shrapnel, pulled the rifle on to his shoulder, and ambled off for the next cover. "A cheerful, misinformed liar," thought I, "but a good man."

For the time at all events my work appeared over. Divisional Artillery took a rest, so far so that I ended by forgetting Divisional Artillery and even the battle. I rested against the naked brown earth, and blinked lazily over the bay, until the sun laid weights on my eyelids. I had no hunger; hunger had departed long since, if it had ever arrived; but I thought of some bubbling stream until my sticky lips opened and shut. It was no good; I had to close my eyes in the end; the lids were too heavy. The last I noticed were dead mules lying along the sea shore. After that the firing went on, but dully; and in the lulls I heard faintly the voice calling through the megaphone: "Angle of sight," I heard. "One-ough minutes right," I heard.

Then all grew closer again: I distinguished musketry and machine guns. The sun blazed less: I could open my eyes. There was Eaves staring, and yes! pelting me with clods of earth. "Wake up," he called out, "and get up with this!"

I opened my eyes wide then, and sat up straight. The sun was much lower down, and fewer ships were in action. Plainly now could be heard the rifle fire. I stood up and blinked. I took the form and started on another climb, and on the way ran into the sergeant-major and Wilkinson coming down. "Lake, you nearly had a new sergeant-major twice to-day. My belt stopped this." And Gardiner held up a bullet in his fingers. Near the dug-out the colonel jumped almost on top of me. The adjutant was just behind. "Yards," he called out, "this battle is already won!"

CHAPTER XII

THE DAY'S BUSINESS

A COUPLE of mornings later, I was pulled out of bed by the telephonist on duty. As usual he had my heartfelt curses, and as usual I bowed to circumstances and sat up.

The night was fine and clear and sharp; and quite silent if one forgot the roll of musketry. No shells passed over to the sea. Standing in the dark and pulling on my clothes, and lastly picking up the overcoat which had been a blanket, I rubbed my eyes wider open and greeted again my old friend the night. There was the bay with many a craft light on its bosom, some winking and winking on for ever; there and there rose up and fell away the folded hills. And the sky was like a giant's blue punch-bowl, picked out from rim to centre with points of golden light. It was an Eastern night; a night for dreams and mysteries and happenings of the long ago.

And yet it was a deucedly cold night too! I fastened the coat collar round my ears, and pulled the woollen cap down to meet it. Over a shoulder went the bandolier, and over that a rifle. With tucker bag at waist I was ready.

Two figures I had noticed moving near the observing station, and, climbing to them, they became Mr. Cliffe and Wilkinson. Wilkinson was loaded up with telephones and tucker bag. The white bag stared through the dark. His head was hidden in a muffler; but he gave me a nod. Both must have been waiting for me, for Mr. Cliffe whispered: "Are you ready, Lake?" and we set off at once. For a space we had to pick a careful way through dug-outs, where sleepers were rolled from head to foot in blankets or rugs, and blocked the road, and snorted at us and groaned. Past all this the advance over the broken hillside was not easy, until we picked up a track leading us up the valley. It seemed some shepherd track made in happier days. Once on the path we went forward at best pace, for dawn was due in half an hour, and by then the trenches must be reached. The valley held snipers, and after daybreak was searched from head to foot by enemy shrapnel. It was no place for mass meetings.

Yes, it was deucedly cold! I stuffed my hands into my pockets, and the others did the same. We marched in Indian file, for the path itself was narrow and full of ups and downs, and we went always at the same hard pace. The road seemed ever rising. Little we said, unless the direction became uncertain, and for the most part our footsteps were all the sounds made.

In the open I had got used to the dark, but

down here in the valleys it was quite impossible to make out anything farther than a yard or two away. The country went up on either side steep and rugged, that much could be seen; and it was covered plentifully with low scrubby bushes, enough to hide an army corps of snipers. The path wound about and about and was much broken in places; and either rain had fallen lately or mountain streams crept down this way, for at one time frequently we splashed through heavy mud or even pools, or were set jumping from tussock to tussock to keep dry shod. As we got higher, matters grew a bit better; and next it seemed we were losing ourselves among the hills.

Mr. Cliffe guided: I was the last of the three. I saw Cliffe dimly four or five yards ahead, a rather small figure moving this way and that among the bushes, putting a hand out sometimes to push aside the branches, more often shouldering the way forward. Then followed Wilkinson on his heels, taller, narrower, and loaded up like a packhorse. Neither the one nor the other ever turned a head, except once when passing a strange object where the path broadened to a road—a mule curled round as if asleep. I wager that mule took a long time waking.

Three or four hundred yards beyond here came suddenly to us the whisperings of a number of voices, voices undecided and even timid. Next moment we were into the tail of a score of men —more there may have been, one could only guess—they formed an uncertain line along the track, and were in full marching order, with their packs up. Either they were coming from or going to the firing line. I poked my head forward to see better, and recognised them as a party of marines who had arrived to reinforce us last evening. They filled the path, obliging us to halt. From the hurried whispers I gathered they had lost the way, and a sergeant was bustling up and down in an attempt to keep all together. They stared at us curiously.

As there was no room we stepped off the path, and pushed through the bushes for a little distance until we were ahead of them. Somebody appeared to be in charge at this end, and Cliffe and he started in muffled conversation. In a few moments I heard Cliffe say: "You'd better hurry, for the place is well dosed with shrapnel at daybreak." Then we went on again.

After this the going became very much stiffer, and though the path still existed, one climbed rather than walked. In a minute or two I forgot to feel cold, in five minutes I was ready to hang my coat on the nearest bush. I was not alone in this: I heard the others labouring. All the time we had been passing marines in groups of threes and fours. They must have been one body moving to the trenches, though now much broken up. In the end we left them all behind, for we travelled quickly in spite of the incline. For already dawn was near: I could not turn to it and say, "Look!"—it was a suggestion rather than a change. But dawn was coming.

We arrived at a spot high up on the hill where the path turned abruptly to the left. Here we halted a few moments and I was very glad. I sat down on the bank and threw open my coat collar. I became aware that a faint greyness had stolen over the world. The change was little, infinitely little; but it was there. On either hand were vague bushes, and the country revealed itself full of shallow trenches and funk-holes, which yawned like endless graves. I grew aware of many men sleeping in the shelter of these, and of tins of beef and bags of biscuit near them, and the ashes of yesterday's fires. I wondered what the men were doing here behind the firing line.

Cliffe sat cross-legged on a tussock, his chin in his hands. He was quite still. All of a sudden he looked round and began to speak.

"Look at these fellows," he said. "I can't make out how it is allowed to go on. Every man there ought to be in the firing line. Instead of that they skulk here all day with plenty of tucker: I'm pretty sure most of them have never seen the trenches at all."

"Why is nothing done?" I asked.

"I believe they are starting to do something, but things have been in a muddle, the battalions mixed up, and no one knows who is dead and who alive. That's the excuse, I suppose. Last evening I was coming down here after that poor Mr. Byers was shot. I spoke to one lot with a fire going, who were filling themselves with bully beef and jam, and asked them what they were doing The fellow I spoke to seemed ready to give cheek, so I pulled out my revolver and he climbed down at once. Later on I met an officer who had lost his way and his men and everything else. He came to me and asked if I could direct him and was nearly incoherent. There was some shrapnel about at the time, and as each shell burst he dived under cover and refused to come out. I spoke to him roughly in the end, though he was senior to me, and finally he started to cry. I left him."

Wilkinson was crouched up on the bank. When Cliffe stopped he began to talk in his rapid way, telling his disgust. As he finished Cliffe got up.

"We had better make another start," he said. "It isn't far."

Even now there was no trace of dawn in the sky; but the greyness I had noticed was more marked and I could make out the leaves on the bushes. It was quite possible to see what was underfoot, and to avoid the numerous trenches zig-zagging about here. We struck the firm path again a little farther on, and from that point the road climbed quickly. We had marched perhaps five minutes, and objects were growing quite clear, when something moved through the sky—there was a bang and a mighty pattering and rustling in the bushes some way behind us, and overhead floated a delicate puff of smoke. The concert had opened. "There goes the first!" Wilkinson cried. "Aye," I said, and Cliffe nodded his head.

We had little breath for remarks and went on as quickly as we could. The half light had penetrated everywhere, although still there were no signs in the sky. But the shrapnel had clapped over our heads, and this was the clock to follow. We turned to the left, we pushed up a fierce bit beside a fresh grave marked by pebbles and a rough cross; we took a half turn to the right, and then I found myself entering a tunnel with no top. The walls sloped down as we went on, until they were no more than four foot from the ground. "Duck," Cliffe said, and set the example, and we ducked for a yard or two, moving at a half run. Again the walls rose high, and soon we could stand upright. I looked about me and found we were in the trenches.

It was now quite light: one could make out everything. This trench seemed seven, perhaps eight foot deep, and must have been a spot of especial importance, as it was well widened out, and farther on it narrowed again to the width of the passage by which we entered. There it took a sharp turn, and one could see no farther.

It was full of men in dull green uniforms, who sat and lay in scooped-out recesses, or stood and blocked the narrow passage. The rifles rested along the trench walls, some with bayonets fixed, some without. It was the first time for a long while I had seen so many Englishmen together, and their faces struck me as kindlier than the Australian face and more simple too. They looked at us with interest when we came in and marched across to the corner reserved for artillery observation. A lieutenant with a brown woollen cap on his head, which made him look like a stage smuggler, leaned from a funk-hole perched rather higher than the others, and asked our business; but beyond that nobody spoke at all.

"Who are you?" the lieutenant asked, leaning round.

"We've come here to observe for the artillery. This is the place we use," Cliffe answered without turning his head. "You must have relieved our fellows in the night."

"Oh, you're Australians! Yes; we arrived last night." And that was all that was said.

We settled ourselves. Wilkinson connected one of the telephones and attached himself to it, and he gave a second one to a rather knock-kneed person who appeared from nowhere. Cliffe began to prepare his lookout a couple of yards away. As for myself, I found the easiest seat I could—there was no work for me until the wire along the valley was cut by shrapnel or spies. A third telephonist joined to Z—Ak, the infantry brigade, lay on his back in a funk-hole beside me. This made the lot of us.

The trenches were topped with a sandbag rampart, and the observer needed to peer through a loophole in them, a risky proceeding. Where we were the rampart was very low, and not more than a foot above our heads, even when we sat down. The sandbags had been dumped on one another and placed a double thickness, and Cliffe and I started to pull them all ways, finishing by leaving several cracks, through one or other of which the whole landscape might be viewed. I took a look through and saw a stretch of desolate country sloping towards some hills. In the grey light it seemed covered with patches of heath and low bushes; and here and there flowers were springing. Not one living Turk could be seen; but the enemy trenches ran parallel with our own at no great distance, and were made out easily by the sandbagged parapets and mounds of newly turned earth.

There was no Turk visible, but in many places appeared the swift movement of a shovel above the parapet, or a heap of earth falling over the bank. The enemy were digging for their lives.

Now that our climbing was over, it grew quite cold again, and I kept on my coat. Cliffe and Wilkinson were of hardier mould, and after a good deal of turning round and thumping and scratching, they made their coats into arm-chair beds, and in this way sought to defeat the uncharitable ground. I settled back in my funk-hole and took stock of things. The musketry on both sides was brisk and loud and continuous; and frequently a machine gun rattled away for a few minutes, ending as abruptly as it began. Near the trench entrance, where the parapet was lowest, bullets plumped over into our opposite bank, and sent up tiny fountains of dust. By now many a shrapnel shell was coming over too, but happily the valley was their target, for they searched it with care from top to bottom.

On the opposite bank, not so far from me, was the grave of one of our fellows. An upright bayonet had been pushed into the ground, and from it hung a soldier's belt. Below was placed a soldier's hat. There were no words of farewell, there were no stones to mark a square of earth; but at long intervals an odd bullet splashed down there and beat an honest tattoo. "My friend," said I; "I vouch there have been bitterer graves than yours."

It was a chilly business and no mistake, sitting up here while the sun climbed tardily from bed. In the end he came over a hill, but the trench walls cut away his beams. The men sat very still, talking in low tones or dozing, and for the present the telephonists were unoccupied, and lay on their sides in a bored manner. To pass the time I decided on a breakfast of jam and biscuits to be washed down with a draught of stale water. Cliffe was taking a peep through one of his holes every now and then; but there were too many stray bullets to make the occupation healthy. He sought the puff of enemy guns.

Without troubling to get up, I unhitched my tucker bag and pushed a hand inside. There was a tin of bully beef, a tin of plum jam, and a lot of the little hard biscuits we had been given before landing. There was nothing interesting, but I started away. I left the beef for later on, and dipped the biscuits into the jam, taking care to bring out more jam than biscuit. I could hear the Englishmen talking among themselves in rather depressed tones. They spoke with a broad accent, and I gathered they were from somewhere up north. "'Tis a bitter place this, choom," I heard one say; and another grunted answer. Thereupon I cocked round my eye and put in a word. "You won't be saying that in a few hours' time," I said. "It's as hot as blazes here."

Everybody looked at me and one or two grinned, but nobody spoke. They seemed to regard the Australians as curious and rather interesting; and they admired us too. It seemed our name as fighters was made when we took the place. I fixed on the nearest fellow. "What part of the old country d'you come from?" "Manchester." And that was all he said. The others hailed from round that part, or from Lancashire at any rate; but conversation was at a discount, and before long I went back to the biscuits and jam.

As time went on, and it drew may be towards seven o'clock, more liveliness came into affairs. The men brightened up and moved about more and cracked heavy jokes. But I yet remained colder than charity, and kept on looking for the sun to climb up and send a little warmth over the parapet. Since our appearance on the scene a man or two had worked away with pick or shovel deepening the trench, and in desperation finally I got up from my funk-hole and took a hand at the work myself. I worked hard and fast until out of breath. I had just given the tools back when the word "Colonel" passed from mouth to mouth, and a party of officers came into the trench on a tour of inspection. The colonel was a middle-aged, middle-sized man in a woollen cap, and he led the way. He had not the least look of a soldier, but all the air of a business man who had never attempted anything more exciting than catching his tram after breakfast. He made several remarks, all of disapproval.

"Why isn't this trench deeper? It was exactly like this when we took over. That's not the way to shovel, man: give me the spade: there, do it like that. Now start, men, start. Don't stand there idling."

The lieutenant was leaning out of his funk-hole with an anxious face. The colonel looked up at him without overmuch kindness in the eye. "A Company is along here, isn't it?" he demanded. "Yes, sir. Straight along. You must keep well down; the trenches are very shallow." "I'm going along there now. Keep these men digging. Don't let them slack. There's been nothing done to-day!" And on the colonel went, bending down and scrambling out at the farther end, his retinue following in silence.

There was no doubt there was a good deal of the amateur in these men. Among other atrocities they had rigged a machine gun in some bushes on top of the parapet to our right hand. The situation was murderous—for us, not the enemy. There was no cover, and to fire the gun meant crouching among the bushes, a sure target for any bullets straying this way. A sergeant was in charge of the gun, and lay on his stomach up there observing the enemy's movements, and sending down reports every few minutes. For some reason the lieutenant in charge made no effort to keep the gun secret, but at frequent intervals ordered fifteen or twenty rounds rapid fire, so that our corner attracted a growing interest from the enemy. A conversation went on after this manner.

"Are you still there, sergeant?"

"Yes, sir."

"Is anything to be seen?"

"No, sir. Nothing important. There is a good deal of digging going on in one place: the men aren't showing; but a lot of dirt goes up."

"Well, give 'em a burst there, it'll keep their heads down; a short burst, not more than twenty, with traversing movement."

A silence followed, and then bang-bang, bang-bang went the gun.

"Any results, sergeant?"

"I'm not sure, sir: I think they've stopped digging."

A few minutes later.

"Anything to be seen, sergeant?"

"Nothing special, sir. I saw a man look over the parapet just now."

"Well, give him a burst. Five or six will do."

Bang-bang, bang-bang, bang-bang went the damned gun again.

Cliffe proved something of a sportsman, and, being so far unoccupied, he had borrowed my rifle and sniped away at intervals through his loophole. I don't know what he saw to shoot at any more than I could discover where all the rifle fire came from. All of a sudden Cliffe called out to me in an excited whisper: "D'you want a shot, Lake? There's an old Turk here poking his head up?" I jumped up, scrambled across to him and took hold of the rifle. Cliffe was staring through a loophole. "Look through here after me," he said. "He's right ahead, about six hundred yards off." I took a long look, but could not pick him up. "D'you see the dead fellow in blue trousers." I picked up the dead Turk all right, lying spread out in a little patch of flowers; and then, thirty yards or more to the right, I did see something move. True enough it was a man. "I've got him," I said. I lifted my head over the parapet to level the rifle; but I had been too long and friend Turk disappeared. I stayed ready some time in case he came back; but he never showed again. Instead the cold morning breeze drifted against my forehead, and climbed about my hair, and I knew a strange feeling looking across that waste to watch our bullets strike the opposite trenches, telling myself the while at any moment Death might stalk from over there and bow to me. "Don't keep your head up too long, Lake," Cliffe said presently. "It isn't over healthy." I took his advice, but settled down where I was in case of fun later on.

Time went along very, very slowly. There was absolutely nothing doing. I tried to talk to Wilkinson and then to Cliffe; but there was nothing to talk about. The Englishmen became more depressed, and finally nobody spoke at all. Yes—I forget the lieutenant—who never lost interest in his gun, and who also called out directions now and then to the men shovelling in the passage way.

The rifle fire continued all the while, and many a bullet knocked up the dust on the opposite bank three or four yards off. The fire had not ceased from the hour of our landing, only up here the noise was sharp and fierce and close at hand.

The enemy shrapnel passed constantly over our heads, though I don't think it did much harm, for it fell in the valley, which was generally empty, except of skulkers, who knew how to look after themselves. Our own guns remained silent. I sat and shivered and felt bored beyond belief.

At last matters mended somewhat.

"You're wanted on the 'phone, sir," Wilkinson said. "Who wants me?" "The colonel, sir."

Cliffe crept the two or three paces towards the 'phone, and put it to his mouth. "Hullo! Hullo there! Yes, Cliffe speaking." A long pause. "Yes, I've got it. C target. Three o'clock right of false ridge. Straight away. Righto, sir."

Back went Cliffe to his peepholes to stare through one of them. "They seem to have woken up down below at last," he said. "The old balloon has spotted some guns in action three o'clock right of the false ridge up there. There's one of them now!" We waited a minute or two, crouching down below the parapet, then Wilkinson, who had the 'phone strapped to his head, said, "Fired, sir."

The voice of a gun travelled from the valley foot, and the same moment a shell swept over our heads and burst in a puff of smoke many hundred yards beyond us. I was staring through one of the cracks. The shot was over the target and rather to the left. "One degree three-ough minutes more right! Shorten corrector four! Drop two-ough-ough! Repeat!" Wilkinson echoed the words: a silence followed. The gun boomed below, and a shell whistled overhead. This time the burst was better. "Drop five-ough! Repeat!" Cliffe called out.

I moved away presently, and tried again to talk with the Englishmen. Nearly all were young, and none seemed overbright. By the time we had exchanged all news, the morning was wearing on; and finally the sun tossed his beams into the trench in a threatening manner.

These were still optimistic days, when we expected the British and French down south to join up with us at any moment. We were always believing to hear their guns, and daily reports came through that they were arriving at such and such an hour. To-day it was to be five o'clock in the afternoon. The village of Krithia had been taken, and Heaven knows what else besides, and at any instant now they ought to come pouring over the top of Achi Baba. The fall of Constantinople was only a matter of days.

The marines were as confident as we Australians, and the belief that the whole affair would be over in a week or two was, I believe, the one thing that bore them up. But they were a home-sick lot at best.

Our guns soon quieted down—shortage of ammunition, no doubt—and Cliffe left his post and came across where the trench was deeper to stretch his legs. The English lieutenant was sitting just above, and the two men drifted into conversation.

I had the luck to find a *Penny Magazine* with a very sentimental love story inside. I carried it to my funk-hole, and made a comfortable bed, and read until the springs of romance welled in me. I fell asleep to dream of governesses and dukes, and incidentally of heiresses who smiled encouragement on broken gunners. When I woke up it must have been midday, as the sun was not far from the centre of the sky, and there was not a foot of shade. I opened a hopeless eye and looked round. All was the same. The men sat in the same places and talked with effort. Cliffe spoke to Wilkinson, and the sergeant lay beside his gun. I yawned and sat up, flapped at the flies and swore.

But why go on? Through endless afternoon things were the same. At times our guns opened and Cliffe observed for them; at times I peeped over the parapet, hoping to snipe a Turk. At times the machine gun rattled away. There was little movement on either side. The armies rested after the big attack. I don't know who was best pleased when the light grew dim and orders came through to return to headquarters.

I met the marines once again. It was on the following afternoon. I had guided Major Felix to the trench; and there we found Sands observing, with Hawkins and Eaves for his telephonists. "Saida," I said to Hawkins, and leaned against the wall beside him.

The same men were in the same places, and digging was going forward as before. The trench had been improved in the night, and was deeper and more secure. But on the other hand I noticed the rifle fire was very heavy, and enemy shells would burst unpleasantly close. Major Felix and I had one or two uneasy moments coming up the valley, so it was disappointing to find we were not to be left alone here.

Eaves sprawled on his back with the receiver strapped to his ear. "'Ullo," he called out lustily when he saw me. "Wot are you doin' 'ere?" I nodded to him and climbed nearer to Hawkins, who sat higher up than Eaves, and more under the lee of the bank.

"How are things?" I said, settling down.

"It's been pretty hot all day," he answered, putting down the transmitter and taking out a cigarette. "This morning they lobbed two or three percussion shells on to the wall over there. They're after the machine gun. It's these fools: they never leave the thing alone for five minutes." He tried to borrow a match and failed. Getting one elsewhere, he went on. "The gun ought to be taken out of the place: they'll have us blown out of the hole in the end."

We yarned away a long time, and I don't know what happened to Major Felix: he disappeared. I stayed on, having no orders to return, and the longer I stayed, the hotter grew the rifle fire. Our own guns in the valley were active, and kept Sands fully occupied peering through his peep-holes, and giving contradictory orders to the telephonists. The Turkish guns were more aggressive than our own. Frequent shells came our way, bursting about fifty yards behind us and dismembering the bushes.

Presently while we sat in silence, for the noise made talking hard, and dreamed of no particular evil, word came down the line that the enemy was massing on our right. This woke the trench up. Two officers of marines were present at the time. One—the lieutenant of yesterday—sat in his favourite seat, the funk-hole commanding this corner of the trench, the other had been giving instructions about the digging. They exchanged excited glances. "Where did the message come from? Who passed the message down?" they demanded in one voice. Someone answered, "The message came by mouth down the trench, sir." "Is that the whole message? Was there anything more? Is anything to be seen?" "I don't know, sir."

The officer in the funk-hole leaned out and looked up towards the machine gun.

"Are you there, sergeant?"

"No, sir," was the answer. "I'm here instead."

"Well, can you see anything? Can you see any special movement?"

There was no reply for a while. Then I heard: "No, sir, I can't see anything particular."

Sands was called into consultation, and his verdict, given in disinterested voice, bore out what the sergeant said. But all the while the fire from both sides was increasing. Bullets plumped time after time into our opposite bank, and a multitude of shells travelled forwards and backwards across the sky. I began to feel warlike. Rapid conversation went on between the officers; but as nothing further happened, excitement died a natural death. We were settling comfortably into our places again when a second message came along. "Enemy massing heavily on our right. Attack expected."

This settled matters. The place buzzed like a beehive. Sands was appealed to again. "Can you see no movements at all from where you are?" "Absolutely nothing," Sands answered in the blandest manner without turning round. A moment afterwards he called to me over his shoulder, "Climb up by the machine gun, Lake, and try to observe the next two shots. I can't pick them up from here. I should try not to get killed if I were you. You probably will be up there."

I did as he told me, and lay flat on my stomach beside the machine gun. There was absolutely no cover, so that I flattened out to the last inch.

I looked across the wilderness of yesterday. Our bullets knocked up the dust along the Turkish line, and our shells broke in delicate white clouds about the sky. One thing I could not see, that was a living Turk. I had not much opportunity to look about, as I had to watch closely the square of ground on which one of our guns was trained. I saw the puff at last and called out the direction, and Sands answered he had picked it up too. The next shot Sands observed as well.

While I was flattened out there calculating how soon a bullet would come that way, a very young lieutenant walked over. "I say, keep down as much as you can," he said, lifting up his face to me, "or you will draw fire on us."

"You blighted ass, what am I doing now?" I thought. "Yes, sir," I said.

The time was about four o'clock, and the men expected to be relieved by another company. In spite of the turn affairs had taken, the men made ready for departure, and quite soon the relieving company arrived and tried to find a way in. They, too, carried fixed bayonets and looked like business. The trench was quite choked up, and I took the hint and climbed into a funk-hole out of the way. Perhaps I was lucky. Officers of the old party were hunting their men out, and confusion was general, when a loud and dull explosion took place quite near, stones and a cloud of dust shot up—and then came silence. A percussion shell had come into the trench. The senior officer was beside me, and he craned his neck forward, and called out in a sharp voice to know who was hurt. "Forbes killed, sir, and two others hit." "Get them away to the doctor, get them out at once: don't block up the way!"

The soldiers pushed themselves against the walls, and the procession went by. The dead man came last. I peered from my funk-hole and looked him in the face. I do not think he was quite dead; but I heard someone say in a stage whisper his back was broken. His face was yellow, and his mouth a little open. Death had not stamped him with nobility.

Yet there was a moment when I forgot the trenches and instead saw another scene. Grey walls were there crossing purple moorland; and in the valley stood slated cottages about an aged church. From there at daybreak the labourers went abroad, and at even the herds came home; and ever there the old men dawdled, and women gossiped by their doors. Year by year the same faces looked on the same faces, but not again would one familiar face be seen.

The new company squeezed against the trench sides, and the old one filed away. The firing from both sides was overwhelming, and our trench bristled with bayonets. For my own part I had seen nothing threatening in the movements of the enemy when up by the gun; but excitement ran high and I caught it. Matters began to look really interesting when a call came for reinforcements on the right. Amid enquiries and commands, a sergeant was sent off at express speed with a party to find out details, and at the same time the trench began to fill up again with the men who had been relieved. Next an officer pushed his way along, revolver in hand. Indecision seemed so great that I began to doubt, in the event of a rush, whether we should hold the trench; and thus I made ready for the worst, fixed a bayonet to my rifle, and prepared to die as becomes an honest gunner. In five minutes back came the sergeant. "They want no reinforcements, sir. There's nothing out of the way doing. They made a demonstration on the right, sir, and attacked our left."

"Hum," thought I.

On the way back to headquarters, we found the top of the valley lined with men upon their bellies, rifles in hand and bayonets fixed.

Another tragedy that corner of the trench showed me.

The marines were relieved next day by an Australian battalion. I was in the trench in the afternoon, and was making the first step on the way home when a shell came in. I swung round towards the uproar, and that moment something struck me on the foot. I looked down and saw a lump of quivering flesh. A captain of infantry had had his neck blown away.

I returned down the valley, sick to death. Shrapnel was spattering in the bushes, and at the cross roads waited three dead and still bleeding mules. I hurried along; but I could not escape that red lump of meat. I could not eat that night: though thirsty I threw away the tea. I rolled into my blankets; but still that lump of flesh was there. Darkness and the cool of night had no power to banish it.

Beastly! Ah, beastly! Ah, very, very beastly!

CHAPTER XIII

A PERILOUS EXPEDITION

SOON after this Sands singled me out as the victim to attend him on a telephone-laying expedition. He warned me overnight, and I felt then a strange unwillingness for the honour; and when the hour arrived, I had not changed my mind. Somewhere about half-past three I was shaken from sleep; and I jumped straight up and pulled on my clothes.

On the way from the dug-out I met Sands wandering round the cook-house like an uneasy ghost. He seemed to be looking for something, and quite ignored my existence for several minutes. But he shot a glance at me more than once out of the corner of his eye, though he spoke no word and went on with whatever he was doing.

At last he came to himself: he pushed hands into his pockets, and started off into the dark. "Come along, Lake," he said casually over his shoulder. And he faded away. Those were the first words he spoke.

I hurried after him, loaded with a hand-reel. We picked a way through the dug-outs down into the valley. Clear starlight was overhead; but it was absolutely dark down there. I had no idea where we were going—no idea of the direction, nor of how far—but this I soon discovered. We were moving towards our right wing.

We took the communication trench which runs from our observing station, and followed it to the end. It emptied us into the foot of the big valley—the one leading to the trenches—but instead of turning up the valley, Sands struck straight across. We passed the Indian camp on our left hand: there was nothing to prove its existence, until the mules began to stamp. Then we picked up a small path winding round the bottom of the hill. I knew it at once; I had passed that way a day or two before. Sands continued to push on a pace or two in advance; and presently without turning his head or making any movement, he called back: "Do you know where A Battery is, Lake?"

"Yes, sir, I was there two days ago."

"Oh; it has moved since then."

"Then I have no idea where it is."

"Neither have I," he said. And he sniggered.

"Are we going to A Battery?" I asked.

"Of course we're going to A Battery. We have to lay a wire from headquarters to their observing station."

"Then why haven't we brought a guide, sir?"

"What do we want a guide for? I was half-way there myself yesterday evening. I have a good general idea where the place is. I was given details last night. Come on, Lake, we mustn't waste time. You can't live where we're going after daybreak." Those were his last words. I began to have misgivings.

The walk soon worked away any drowsiness left in me, and I found myself wishing we had been on a more peaceful errand and in a more charitable land, for the night, or the morning rather, showed us countless wonders along the way. It was warmer than I had yet known it at that hour, too warm in fact for the hills we must scramble up; and the stars in rows and rows looked down on us with their unreadable eyes. One might look right into the heavens until one blinked and turned away, and one would discover still more distant golden worlds watching and watching and giving no sign.

The little winds which met us ran in and out of the bushes, flip-flapping the smaller leaves and just stirring the larger; and the scents of the few spring flowers, which had already opened their faces to the world, floated down from somewhere or other with a strength and sweetness the day never left them. The very pebbles seemed to scatter musically before our feet.

The dew was heavy on the bushes, and splashed my forehead and my hands with great cool drops. I caught at the leaves and rubbed my hands in them, and so had a first wash for the day. The musketry rolled on, and the lamps were a-winking in the bay, saying that on land and sea man was abroad; and I heard no sounds nor caught a movement of beast or bird of night. I looked and listened too. Yet doubtless many a keen pair of eyes gleamed at us from the roots of the bushes; but man was passing, man who had come in his hordes and had made the solitude unholy. The night called with stars and dew and silence; but we pushed on to prepare fresh destruction.

We came to a steep and narrow gully which turned at right angles from the path. "This is the shortest way to the old position of A Battery, sir," I said.

"Well, lead the way, Lake."

"But you said they had moved, sir."

"Go on, Lake, lead the way; it will bring us somewhere near them. One way is as good as another."

He had no idea where the battery was! Good God!

I led the way. The path was quite easy for a hundred yards and even farther; but afterwards it was necessary to clamber up some difficult cliffs. The undertaking in the dark was going to be severe. I came to a full stop and turned round.

"This is the way," I said, and pointed up. Sands eyed it pensively.

"Is that the only way?"

"There is another longer but much easier road which sweeps round the hill. Shall we take that?"

"Yes, we shall. Hurry up, Lake. It's late already: the sun will soon be up. We'll be dead men if you waste time here much longer."

His words sounded alarming; but he did not seem much worried at the prospect.

Complete darkness favoured us still; but dawn would not long delay. I, too, considered it was time to hurry. We were back again on the main path in very few minutes, following it over the shoulder of a hill. The climb was stiff and soon made us steady the pace. Wherever we went the country was the same, covered with low bushes and destitute of a single tree of any proportions. On the summit of the shoulder, the path turned to the left and climbed up to the top of the hill. I went on along it, for it led directly to the old position of A Battery. But Sands stopped, and I noticed him peering down into the next valley. "No, this is the way," he said, all of a sudden. "I'm pretty certain the guns have been taken somewhere over here." Forthwith he started along a road which dipped straight down, and looked to run directly for Gaba Tepeh.

There was a wide view of the ocean from here, and from the waters drifted a salty breeze. It was a message that day was at hand. Whether Sands discovered poetry in that scene or not I cannot say; but he stood still a moment with his head on one side eyeing the shadowy waters. The reverie lasted brief time. "It will be light quickly now, Lake," he said. "If we don't find the guns, we shall probably be dead in half an hour."

In his voice there was neither anxiety nor even interest; he made the statement as one might remark the evening was excellent for a walk.

We said no more all the way down the slope.

I knew now he had no idea where we were, where we were going, nor what was to happen to us. And I knew also that Gaba Tepeh was straight ahead. I saw us lost among the wire entanglements, waiting to be sniped like crows when light should come that way. A tender sadness crept into my heart. No more for me the lambs would frolic, no more the jackass would laugh or the magpie jodel; no more, with joyous bark, would the family hound meet me at my gate. Such joys were for others. I dropped a silent tear.

A stiff hill rose directly ahead, and the world was vaguely grey with the approach of dawn. Sands looked at this hill, looked hard at it, and once or twice threw a glance at me from the tail of his eye. Finally he swore feebly and started to climb it.

I do not know whether the road was old or not, it was wide and seemed smooth enough; but the sappers may have made it. They seemed able to throw up roads where they liked.

I went to the side of the way, and helped myself along by pulling at the bushes. The last poetic feelings left me here, and in their place came sentiments of utmost venom towards Sands. For his own part he said nothing at all, but just breathed heavily, perspired and toiled on.

Some distance up, the road circled backward and lost some of its steepness, and I could see that, though we never reached our goal, we should find ourselves presently in the neighbourhood of home. I began to take heart.

After we had gone some distance and the minutes had hurried by and the landscape was taking form round us, the path crossed at right angles a road, and to my astonishment the new track bore fresh gunmarks. Sands gaped a moment, like myself in doubt, and too overcome for speech; but not long was such a veteran nonplussed. He looked me calmly in the face and said, easily, "I knew it was somewhere just about here, Lake. We follow the road right up. A Battery will be somewhere on top of the hill. We must hurry: the shrapnel will start any minute now." He set the example. What could I say to such luck? I bowed my head and meekly followed.

We pursued the wheeltracks up the hill; but could not keep up the pace. Farther on we ran into a camp—sappers, I think they were—and the guard told us guns had passed by during the night. It was now twilight, and the country was distinguishable. A hundred yards farther on we followed the gun tracks off the main path; and then, round a corner, we came on a gun and a waggon and a camp of artillerymen. A few men were up and about; but many were rolled still in the blankets. The guard told us the battery was not far away, and gave directions. In no time we were among the communication trenches. They ran this way and that, so that we were constantly asking the way. Sleeping men lay along the bottom of the trenches, and it was hard to avoid them all; in truth, more than one string of oaths followed our progress. Finally, we came on the battery observing station, where was Major Felix with several men. I took a seat on a stone in the background while Sands explained his errand. I do not know what he said, but the major's face failed to light up with welcome. Presently Sands beckoned to me with a jerk of the head. "We are laying the line to here," he said, as we came up. "We have to find the drum now. Jones and I brought it half-way up the valley last night."

So we were only starting operations!

The battery was on top of a large flat hill, and the guns were not yet properly dug in. Gangs of men were shovelling hard as we arrived, and others were dragging behind them masses of bushes for covering the guns from aircraft observation. Everyone worked at top speed; but even so, I could see they would never get matters finished by daybreak. Sands began to lead me over a stretch of waste country, the usual waste land in fact—stunted bushes and coarse grasses, and here and there young flowers springing up. Countless exploded Turkish shells lay among the grasses; and in frequent places the turf was torn up by the heavy fire which swept there from time to time. This must have been the place Sands had in his mind when he prophesied our destruction at dawn. But morning had broken quietly with the old roll of musketry and nothing more.

My gallant guide appeared to have lost his bearings again, for he kept no direct course. Once we passed a dead infantryman among the grasses. The body had been overlooked, and was fast decaying in the fierce suns, and the morning air was tainted for yards around. I was glad to get by. Sands looked long and hard at the unpleasant sight; but he made no comment. Presently I found we had come to the head of the gully we started to ascend earlier in the morning. "Here we are," Sands said, coming to a halt. "The drum is somewhere down there," and he waved his hand about the horizon. I looked down and realised the dance he had led me.

The country was difficult, but daylight helped us to find the best tracks. We stood a minute or two planning the descent down the ravines, and looking for the best passages through the tangled undergrowth. Presently forward we went, slipping and sliding a great part of the way. There were times even when progress was made by climbing down rather than by walking. Well, on we went, sliding and slipping and scraping our shins, and then, as suddenly as we had come upon the gun tracks, we came across the drum. I was ready for Sands to say he knew it had been there all the time; but he was occupied finding breath and made no remark. We rested a little while with the fresh breezes moving about us. Daylight had found a way into every recess; and one or two venturesome insects were abroad already, and one or two birds were singing. Here and here, in ones, twos, in threes, were the rude graves of fallen soldiers. A couple of twigs bound to form a cross marked one, a piece of board with date and initials a second, an upright rifle a third.

Already the dwarf hollies were closing round them: already the stunted laurels were bending over them.

Then began the climb back. It had been difficult before, and the drum nearly settled matters. However, on the way we found an easier if longer track, and half up the hill the wire on the big drum ended, and we used the hand-reel for the remainder of the distance.

It did not take so long then, though we stopped at all the tallest bushes and tied the wire to them. A Battery observing station was deserted on our arrival, and we fastened the wire to the 'phone and came away.

While we passed the open space on the hilltop for the third time, and as I had just muttered thanks for the morning calm, there came a whizz and a bang right overhead. A puff of smoke curled away in the high sky. The shell had missed us by a few yards. Sands stopped, and I knew at once he was going to say something worthy of himself.

"You know, Lake, I am very disappointed we came here. I wanted to see a real battle. This is only a sniping expedition."

I said not a word. Farther on he stopped to adjust the wire. He took it in his hand and began bounding into the air in an attempt to throw it over the top of a high shrub. I went up to him, but was waved off. "You can go on, Lake, and get some breakfast. I shall follow in a minute or two."

I sauntered on, expecting him to overtake me

very soon. A wall of cliff rose in front, and just there the platform bent abruptly round it. I strolled to the end of the path and turned the corner, and came in full view of the ocean.

Last shadows had gone, nor did a star remain in the sky; and the thousand pure lights of the young morning fell about the ocean in cascades of silver and blue. All over the place small glad waves were bobbing—wavelets of silver, wavelets of azure; and on the broad bosom of those radiant seas rode the noblest fleet that ever had sailed that way. Ships of war were there, and ships which had grown ancient in piping days of peace: leviathan and cockleshell waiting alike the call of morning.

The sun still lay abed, yet the world of foliage between me on my hilltop and the sea moved in a million shades of green as the breezes passed among them. It was like a great green hymn of praise going up to God.

And scores of tiny smoke clouds climbed from the breakfast fires along the beach, and at sea a hundred funnels were a-smoking too. Up they rose in tones of blue, from blue they put on a coat of grey, and climbing on, faded into the joyous morning lights.

Along the blue horizon was heaped a mountain of snowy clouds. So still it lay, so purely white it shone, it seemed the barrier to an enchanted land. I watched, and as I watched the sun rose up from bed and with his foremost glances melted the virgin bank. To right, to left it rolled apart, and lo! clad in the splendours of the dawn—came forth the mountain isle of Imbros. I bowed my head as one who stands on holy ground.

Saffron and rose and purple and violet, and all the other shades of nature's magic paintbox, floated or trembled or rippled about those still peaks. And film by film the virgin shroud about their feet lifted and lost itself in the sheen of shimmering seas.

I bowed my head, and would have put my shoes from off my feet.

Sands's step crunched among the rocks. I glanced round and found him level with me. Straightway I forgave him the expedition. He had shown me this.

CHAPTER XIV

DEATH AND THE BATTERY

WE had yarned outside the cookhouse since the midday meal. Oxbridge was there, and Stone, and Prince; and one or two others, I think. We sat in the open on biscuit tins or stones, or whatever was handy; for the day was sunny and quite mild. There was nothing to do, and we talked on and on.

The tireless musketry fire rolled from the valley head, and enemy shells still burst haphazard along the beach and over the sea. But for an hour or more headquarters had been free from such attention, and that was all that concerned us. Instead of pondering over shells, old Sam Oxbridge had grown homesick again, and was holding forth now on a theory of his own—that after six months' active service, the Government would send home all men wanting to go. His reasoning seemed a bit faulty; but he convinced himself.

In spite of the lazy shelling, the beach was thick with the usual crowds. And the bay was full of vessels. Old Sam stood up at last, tall and with a stoop, and remarked all this with unappreciative eye. I went on stirring Welsh rabbit in a mess-tin lid, all my hopes fixed on it. The fire was nearly done, and called for new wood, and the cheese was simmering. It was a toss up which would win.

Sam's arguments had not impressed us much, but somehow or other we stopped talking, and one looked out to sea, and one cleaned his pipe, and I went on cooking. We were all sick of the business, that was the truth. Men climbed up and down the hillside, moving to their dug-outs and that sort of thing; fragile clouds passed across the sun and darkened its face a few moments; the breeze rustled over the few bushes spared by the cook's axe: such things I saw while I knelt and watched the Welsh rabbit through critical moments. Old Sam still stared into the distance, I noticed that too, and just then a gust of wind filled my eyes with smoke, and with an oath I sprang up behind him. As my eyes cleared he turned to move away, and that instant something struck him with a hard, dull sound, and he breathed out a long-drawn "Oh!" and threw his hands forward and fell upon the ground. He got up again and fell down once more. A shell had burst along the hill.

The doctor, who saw it happen, ran up, and we carried Sam under shelter of the cookhouse and laid him on his back. His eyes were shut, and his breathing was loud and difficult, and already he was turning a horrid grey. The Red Cross orderlies joined us.

We, who could not help, drew back out of the

way under the shelter of the cookhouse walls. The doctor leaned forward and pulled up Sam's shirt, baring his chest. Below the heart was a small red mark. A second shell burst upon the hill, and a third farther along. They were ranging for us again.

None of us said a word, and only one man moved: the doctor was taking a syringe from its case. First he held it against the light, and next pushed it into the dying man's arm.

A fresh burst of fire swept the hillside, and each man looked to himself wondering if he were next. Shells began to fall about us. They began to fall fast and to burst close around us. Soon I was looking at the sea through a wall of red dust. We huddled back against the cookhouse, and Stone's heart went thump, thump, against my chest, and he lay as still as a mouse. Prince, on the other side of him, had lost his head altogether, and, as the shells burst, threw his arms out to push them off. The dust rose thicker and thicker, and finally the sun shone through it in the form of a sullen red ball.

We watched the coming of Death. Sam never moved again, except once when he turned his head slightly; but the unnatural breathing went on, went on and grew more feeble. The doctor sat with his back to us, and his head bowed between his shoulders. He moved seldom; seldom, I think, lifted his eyes from the dying man. By him the orderlies knelt, huddled together to get what cover they could; and the shells would swoop down with a roar and a scattering of the dust. Nobody said anything that I can remember, but time passed and left us watching the still figure, and listening to the horrible breaths.

At last the firing passed farther along the slope, and the dust settled once more. The adjutant came down from his dug-out. "Is he badly hit?" he said, looking down and jerking his head.

"The bullet went in below the heart. He is still alive, and that is about all."

The adjutant raised his eyebrows, nodded, and went away. We became silent again.

Hawkins came back from the valley next, and passed by us. I thought he was staring at Sam, but he never saw him. The doctor spoke at once. "You had better get under cover, Hawkins. They have been dusting things up round here just now." "Yes, I saw that," Hawkins said, with a laugh. And he curled up in his dug-out.

Presently the waiting was over. Death had won—the last trench was taken, the final fortress stormed. Captain Lawler got to his feet, and spoke to the orderlies. "Is the stretcher here?"

I looked into Sam's face and an old thought came back to me. Death is not often beautiful. Here was no heroic end; here was no bold gaze, which told of past duties well done. Nothing of that kind, nothing. But, instead, a silly smile where the mouth dropped, and a little blood upon the palate, and a skin turning yellow and blue. Not heroic, my friends; not beautiful!

I stared down at Sam while they covered him with a blanket. Thoughts I would have put aside at that place and at that hour came to me.

Friend Sam, you were rather "a rotter"—weak and easy to lead. Life owed you more years; but they would have been years without profit. Now you have died at the start of life, and others following will remember your sacrifice and take heart. You could have done no better thing. Methinks you will sleep soundest here, where the cliffs climb up by Sari Bahr.

If you should step it out afar
To the pebbly beach of Sari Bahr,
Full many rude graves you'll find there are,
By the road the sappers drove there.

Crooked the cross, and brief the prayer,
Close they lie by the hillside bare,
Captain and private, pair by pair,
Looking back on the days they strove there.

Aye, still they lie, their work all done,
Resting at ease in the soil well won;
And listening hard for Gabriel's gun,
To spring up and salute as behove there.

CHAPTER XV

ROUTINE

DAY and night, night and day; they came and went again like the pendulum of an eternal clock. They brought us varying fortunes such as a soldier learns to receive in meekness: they grew into weeks and brought the first awful breaths of summer.

Much had happened since the first wonderful rush. Our footing was secure, trenches were deep and safe and numerous, and communicated with support galleries where reinforcements rested. Our guns were in position, every man boasted his own funk-hole. The army was much increased; the wilderness was peopled.

Our field artillery brigade had moved headquarters from the beach to a hillock near the head of Shrapnel Valley. The change left us near the firing line, but, even so, few shells came our way. Several more of our fellows were landed now, and the staff was nearly complete again. But Death had interested himself in us, his eye had looked this way, his fingers had felt among us. First Oxbridge went, then old Bill Eaves followed him; then went Lewis, with the face of a girl. I have told you of Oxbridge; I shall tell you of the others in good time.

That officer of parts, Mr. Sands, was ashore the first day, ahead of anyone, I believe. He was forward observer for the artillery. We saw nothing of him for two or three days, and then he appeared out of the wilderness in most piteous condition. He was painted all over with dust, he was unshaven and unwashed; his clothes had never been off and were crumpled and torn, and a boot had lost its heel. He ran at the nose and seemed worn out, having the look of a man far gone with hunger and thirst. No scabby and dinnerless pariah prowling the streets of Constantinople was in more awful case.

I was doing nothing when he turned up, and I must perforce keep an eye on him. Always I had a liking for the fellow. For whatever his iniquities, Sands was no coward. And if a man be game, he atones for much; when death arrives, can he but take up his hat and say firmly, "I am ready," will not many items be wiped from the slate? And so I doubt not Sands's Valkyrie waits him in Valhalla.

But down below here he found sorry welcome. The colonel spoke a few sentences and dismissed him with abrupt nod, leaving me sure he had messed our shooting. The other officers said nothing at all. So he emptied somebody's water-bottle, and next sat down without a word, as though no more fight remained in him.

But after midday tucker he perked up, for was

he not Sands the irrepressible? He found a handkerchief somewhere and then came over in my direction, and sat down affably enough to smile his Sandslike smile.

"You're still alive?" he said, looking on to the ground, and picking a leaf from a bush to crumple in his hand.

"Yes, sir, I'm all right."

He did not look at me at all, it was a trait of his; but he showed no signs of going away, and sat on crumpling the leaf to powder. All at once he said, "How d'ye like this?"

"It's better than Mena." He answered with a kind of chuckle. "What sort of time have you had, sir?" He said nothing, but sniggered again. "You were over pretty early, weren't you, sir?"

"Oh, yes, Lake, pretty early," he answered. "But I wasn't in the rush up the hill. I was with the brigadier then."

"The infantry seem to have done all right," I said. "You can see their packs at the bottom of the hill over there, where they threw them off."

"Yes, the Third did all right," he went on, after a pause. "But you know it wasn't the great affair it was made out to be. We were expected to land lower down, on the flat where the entanglements are. But there was some mistake or other, and we were put off here. The Turkish army was lower down, and there was only a machine gun detachment on the beach. After that had been rushed, there was practically no resistance until we were at the top of the hill. By then the Turks had brought their men up, and when we got to the open country and came properly under fire, our men began to waver and fall back, and that was how so many officers were lost, rallying them. Afterwards they advanced too far, and pushed on nearly into the Turkish camp, and as the reinforcements were not there, they had to retreat under heavy fire, and so the losses happened." He snivelled as he finished, and as afterthought brought out the handkerchief.

This seemed a more likely story than the other one. The scrub lay on the hills as thick as hairs on a mat, and no men could rush through it, and no enemy could see to shoot them if they did. The first story was a fine one, but this second more true. Sands took up his tale again.

"You hear every man say there are only a hundred men left of his battalion, and that he is the last man of his platoon, and that kind of thing; but, of course, it isn't so. The battalions lost themselves the first day, they're all mixed up, and until there's a chance to reorganise a bit, thousands will be missing."

We sat a long time without speaking again; but at last Sands looked sideways at me.

"Lake, next time you are down at the beach, do you think you could find me a pair of boots somewhere? These are done for." And he pushed forward the one with the heel gone. "You ought to be able to get something at the hospital or the morgue. One boot will do if you can't get a pair."

He looked so broken down, and yet said so little of his troubles, that my heart went out to him, and I answered gladly enough I would do what I could. Next morning I was passing the hospital, and, remembering him, looked inside. The picture was not pleasant, and there seemed no boots about. I went on to the quartermaster, and, after a little haggling, got a new pair. Away I started and dangled them before Sands.

"You've got a new pair!" he exclaimed, getting up in a hurry. "You're the most wonderful man, Lake. I never could have got them."

"I couldn't get any laces, sir," I said.

"That doesn't matter in the least. These are splendid. I would willingly give ten shillings for them." And he looked at me in a sort of what-about-it way, and then dropped the subject. Thus it came about that Sands regained his respectability.

In a week or two, the whole face of the country was changed, and the army had settled down into a daily routine. The scrub was thinning under the demands of cooks for firewood, and definite roads pierced the main valleys and linked them together, while paths crawled over the hills wherever there were headquarters or gunpits, or whatever else you like. The feeling of great adventure was done with.

On first days I had been up some of those valleys, pushing a way through the scrub if I left the track by a yard. And all the way one would tumble on relics of the first advance. It sorrowed my heart to look about. Boxes of ammunition had been thrown down in the undergrowth, tens of thousands, aye, hundreds of thousands of rounds spilled about for the dews to damp and blacken. Cases of jam, big yellow cheeses, sacks of bully beef lay here, unclaimed except by such runaways as were on the lookout for a dinner. Once I found a dead donkey loaded up as he had started on the journey. At every dozen paces one passed rifles and web equipment and endless other things, some damaged in the great game, true; but much just spoiling there for the want of picking up.

And the scrub held other secrets. As you peered among the shadows you might happen on strange and grisly objects lying even stiller than the leaves in the hot noon: horrid black and swollen figures, causing you to turn and push for opener spaces. Or a short-lived, sickly wind might come drifting over, warning of yet other spots to be left alone.

I would not have you think we were careless with our dead, and left them as they died, but some fell in lonely places, and some lay under enemy fire where the search parties could not go. Few only were left thus unattended. In strangest, most difficult, most wayward places little graves had found a way: here one alone, now a community of them; each with simple marks which spring was hiding, and which winter would wash presently quite away.

Australia alone had not left marks for passage. At one time there were many Turkish prizes for him who sought. Choked rifles, a clip of pointed cartridges, a belt, a water-bottle: any of these were there to point out the path of battle. And of empty shell-cases and fuse-caps there was no end: one never troubled to turn them over.

Springtime had come along, the hour of love-making was at hand, and tiny birds played hide-and-seek through all this ruin. When we tired of our furies, and the guns awhile shut their mouths, you could hear the birds singing and singing, so swollen were they with love. I have crouched in odd corners of that playground waiting for an outbreak of shrapnel to pass, and I have seen the happy hurry-scurry in the twigs, and I have thought—but what does a soldier with thinking? A soldier draws pay to act.

These times I speak of were in early days, before the army had landed and changed wilderness to a peopled city. As soon as the hour of pause came, fatigue parties were sent abroad to bring in the wasting material. And curio hunters, and such people as cannot pass an object without taking possession, cleaned up whatever was overlooked. At one time there was regular trade with the navy, who gave a loaf of bread for an empty Turkish shell-case. Presently there grew up large fenced graveyards, with level rows of graves and a wooden cross at the head of each. The greenery was thinned, there were easy ways to the stiffest points, and many of the birds went off to happier lands. So, much that was romantic departed.

I had a central funk-hole—near headquarters and near the cookhouse. I had a balcony, eighteen inches high maybe, and from a seat I dug there one could look across the sea into the eye of the setting sun. There was a tiny path just above the funk-hole, used by everyone coming from the valley top to headquarters; and all who went that way sent a trickle of dirt into my bed. Some honest spade work might have mended matters, but it was a big affair, and I was too lazy ever to begin. A melancholy bush grew by the path, but from it I received no shade; and I was driven to rig a shaky overhead cover of waterproof sheets, the spoils of early days. This awning kept off the sun a little; but the space below had a sickly heat when there was no breeze. At night I took down the cover; and by leaning on an elbow, I could look over the sea, or stare up to watch the stars turning in the skies.

We were always certain of our dinners now, and there was plenty to eat, though, to speak truth, the stuff was sufficiently uninteresting. And so—as all the others were doing—we of the Staff settled down to hum-drum everyday affairs.

Much of the desert training went for nothing. We had not a horse ashore. The guns were man-handled to this or that position, and dug in. An overhead cover of sandbags went up, and heavy sandbagged ramparts grew around. And there the gun stayed for days: it might be for weeks. From first to last we never wagged a flag; all lines of communication were kept by telephonists. The signallers sat down to an office girl's duty. The staff telephonists dug a funk-hole, quite a roomy affair, with seats and a step down. All lines came together here, so that the place grew into a regular exchange with switchboards and other affairs. You would always find two or three fellows at home, and a heap of Melbourne papers in the corner. The fellows were ever ready for a yarn, and could give you beach information for trench news. A fatigue party of batmen made daily trips to the beach for rations.

Now there was scarcely a horse on land, mules performing the transport work and mountain battery work. So it came about that haughtiest generals tramped the rounds as any vulgar private. And among the hapless horsemen left horseless to toil the hills may be counted Gunner Lake. Galloper I remained in name only. I came to foot it behind the colonel on every excursion, and as he was restless as the wind, and stayed unrebuffed by sun or mountain height, I grew to be known as periscope carrier from Walker's Ridge to The Wheatfield. We could tell you of the end of every winding of every trench; and on the moment could upend the periscope, and point you whatever you wanted—Lonesome Pine or Jackson's Jolly, Collins Street or the Chessboard: it was all the same to us. And we could do more than that. We could point to the hidden battery at C; we could show you the puff of the gun on Turk's Hump; and could put your eyes on the V-shaped piece on the skyline where lurked the captured seventy-five.

In the beginning our guns had little luck. Truth to tell, they were at disadvantage. The country was no field gunner's country. First we lacked the horses, and must move the guns by means of imprecations and our sweat. Next the lay of the country was wrong; and space so lacked that we must shoot from the pockets of our infantry. This drew fire on neighbouring trenches, and the infantry loved us accordingly.

The colonel was a restless spirit, loving the society of his guns as should an honest gunner. First thing each day he would make his bath of a spoonful of water, standing up as naked as the ground below, and rubbing himself over in brisk fashion. To the bath he added a shave; and while he dressed he talked over the telephone to Divisional Artillery or the batteries. Then we began the rounds. The colonel would get up, tuck the periscope under his arm with a "Come along, Lake," and lead the way up the path over my dug-out. Close on his heels I followed. A few yards on he would hold back the periscope without turning round. Sometimes he might say, "You are younger than I am." Frequently he said nothing at all. Level country or hill land, he went always at an eager pace.

Each morning we drew the same cover, starting on B Battery preserve, and ending there again midday or later.

The path above my funk-hole led by steep pinches to the head of Shrapnel Valley, one of two main valleys piercing these hills. Shrapnel Valley and Monash Valley they were named; and Shrapnel Valley was the centre of our position. Once all had been wilderness as I have told; then appeared half-way a couple of barrels where the sappers had tapped for water, and about the same time a field dressing station came into being across the way. The position was important, and soon infantry brigade headquarters claimed the top, a New South Wales battalion headquarters kept house alongside, and we gunners prospected lower down. Dug-outs, cookhouses, and officers came in our wake, and in no time a primitive township grew up with suburbs wandering downhill towards the beach.

As often as not the colonel made a first call at infantry brigade headquarters, for we must pass it on the way. There was a notice board without; and I read Reuter's telegrams while the colonel went inside.

Now, General Runner, the infantry brigadier, was a tough customer, and an Indian man, I think, from his ribbons and the colour of his face. His A.D.C. was trained to jump at the wrinkle of an eyelid or the bristle of a moustache hair. What his staff thought of him I don't know, but he was liked well enough by the men. He had a curious droop of an eyelid; and when he shot his savage glances at you, he seemed to shut his eyes. He may have had a liver or he may not; but this I know, I should be sorry for his butler when the coffee was cold of a morning.

Like most of the big men, he was for ever poking about the trenches, nor was he chary of a risk. He was a true periscope fiend, holding the periscope well above the parapet so that every sniper for hundreds of yards was potting away. Possibly periscope casualties were his vanity. One morning the periscope was struck sideways. The general's head was just below the parapet, and the bullet passed an inch or so over his cap. He cocked his wicked eye up—he had quick movements like a bird—and looked at the holes in the tin case. "Bullet through the periscope, sir?" came a toady's voice. The brigadier twisted about his head, and looked down. Then followed a noise between a chuckle and a choke, and back he went to his observation.

When the colonel and I made an early call at infantry brigade headquarters, the general would be at breakfast or in his office. He had built a table of a sort, and he sat at the head of it, often in the open air, with his staff before him. There was nothing special to eat; but the company lived in a civilised fashion, which keeps a man alive. On the colonel's approach, the general would look up. "Good morning, Jackson," he would say, passing a hand over his hair in a way of his; and then he would pucker his face and squint, for the sun was always in his eyes. "Morning, sir." Brigadier and colonel would talk then for a few minutes, the brigadier in a strong high-pitched voice, which generally had last word. It was said he was hard to turn from his opinion; and I believe he had strange artillery ideas. However, argument and explanation did not delay his breakfast. He chewed on with easy indifference. Presently the colonel would come away, not always best pleased, and we would start up a very stiff pinch which took us to the top of the valley. There it was the trenches ran away to right and left, excepting for a space of twenty yards maybe, where the empty waterway down the valley began. This opening was protected with wire entanglements and sandbag ramparts.

One or two really good dug-outs were about here, places with plenty of sawn timber gone to their making, with roofs of corrugated iron and sandbags, and curtains of old sacking to keep away the sun. There were always rough tables in such places, and plenty of upended packing cases for chairs. One can tell a man's character from his funk-hole.

There was a cookhouse down in the bed of the creek, where a cook compounded savoury messes from pretty hopeless materials. I have sat on the bank above on a red-hot afternoon, wondering how he found the spirit to go on at the job. That cook grew a beard in time; but he never left it to straggle as did other men. It was pointed and trimmed. He talked to nobody, and I wondered what he thought about down there. Maybe he cooked to forget his miseries. He cooked and he kept shut his mouth, which was all asked of him. A fellow can grow into a hero by shutting his mouth on a remorseless campaign of this kind.

There was another dug-out near by, where later on lived among bombs and empty boxes the sergeant of the trench mortars. He was a small man, and middle-aged, with sad eyes. He was a man of birth, a gentleman, and was said to have a history. I wondered what he thought of sitting there alone after putting his mortars to bed.

Once we dragged a couple of guns behind these trenches, but we had no luck with them. Two sergeants were sniped before a shot was fired. The guns went back to the valley bottom afterwards, and stayed there; but the colonel was never truly content.

At the valley head you turned to the right hand for B Battery observing station, and for the left hand did you want Clayton's trenches where Sands observed. Always we turned to the right. The way was through a deep cutting with scooped-out seats on either side, where often sat two stretcher-bearers reading papers or playing cards. Other fellows would be here too to gain the few yards of shade and the slight draught caused by the high, close walls. They gambled for ever for cigarettes.

Beyond the gamblers began the trenches, and near by at their mouth was B Battery observing station. I have described it before: it had been held by the marines. The spot was much improved since then, was wider and safer; besides, the enemy had lost interest in it. The telephonists grilled in the sun there, for as elsewhere in this barbarous country there was no spot of shade. As often as not Major Cannister, the battery commander, was with his men.

"Good morning, Cannister," the colonel would say coming up, glad to stand still after the climb.

"Good morning, sir," Cannister would answer. And then they saluted one another, and Cannister would come away from the big periscope tied against the parapet, leaving the sergeant-major or somebody else to watch in his place. And the colonel and he would sit side by side on the hot earth and exchange latest news. As a start the colonel's cigarette case came into sight. He would open it and eye bitterly the weekly dole of Woodbines. "Have one?" he would say, holding open the case. "I'm getting some real cigarettes this week, thank God!" And he would take one himself and light it, and stare at the opposite wall with his keen eyes. "Anything doing this morning, Cannister?"

"Nothing at all. I put a round into 'C' half an hour ago, that's all." Cannister never could resist "C."

"Be careful, Cannister, we can't afford to throw away a round. We're cut down to five rounds this morning. Five rounds a day! Good God! And this is supposed to be a war!"

"Short of ammunition again?" came from Cannister.

"Yes, and after all the talk. The old man rang me up this morning, and said five was our limit. He had done all he could, but it was no use. They're saving up for something. We're going to have a real battle in a day or two. Think of it, Cannister, a real battle, with noise and smoke and two or three extra rounds to fire off. It will be quite like a story book. It will be a column in the *Argus* for us. Think of it, Cannister. Think of it."

Generally Cannister thought pretty hopelessly of it. He would cross his legs and smile and say nothing. But the colonel could say enough for two.

"What do they bring us here for," he would

begin again impatiently, "if we mustn't fight? One might be in Melbourne now, where one could get a drink and a decent cigarette. How much ammunition has come with the new howitzers, do you think? Fifty rounds! They're limited to a round a day or something! Good God! Why don't we shoot off all we've got, and then pack up the guns and send them home, and go to Hell like gentlemen!"

Cannister would answer nothing.

"The brigadier has started fussing again. I don't know what he expects us to do. He is on again about Mortar Ridge gun. I've told him a dozen times it's a New Zealand target. God knows what the New Zealanders are doing! They never open their mouths, or if they do, they shut up again at the first return shell."

So the talk went forward until it was time to move on. Then the colonel took a final look round through his periscope. "I'm going to C Battery and then to A. Ring me up if you want me." Colonel and major saluted. We marched off through the trenches then, making good pace along less crowded bits; but often pulling up to look at that or this Turkish work from this or that position, or stopping to gather latest news or only to pass the time of day.

A trench may be romantic, but it makes a thankless home. These trenches were deep and narrow, and quite safe from rifle fire, and pretty secure from shrapnel. Of course now and then there were accidents. A fellow would keep his head too long at a loophole and get sniped, or a bullet would come through a badly filled sandbag and settle some poor devil's account. It would mean the call: "Pass the word for stretcher-bearers: stretcher-bearers wanted on the right!" and the men gambling at the entrance would hurry along. There would be a few minutes' delay while the dead man was wrapped up in a blanket or waterproof sheet, and put on the stretcher together with his pack and other belongings, and then began the tiresome journey to the beach. Someone would get hold of a shovel and cover up the bloodstains, and that was the end of the affair. You might hear them say: "Smith's gone. Bad luck, weren't it? A bullet copped 'im in the 'ead. 'E wasn't a bad bloke." Sun and thirst, indifferent food, and a dog's sleep leave little energy for regretting.

The trenches zig-zagged all the way, that, part being lost, the enemy's fire could not enfilade for any distance. Where fellows had not stretched blankets overhead by pinning them to the walls with bayonets, there was no spot of shade, the sun stared in on to the baked earth and searched out every corner. Sometimes one discovered attempts at comfort—seats, little fireplaces, shelves for ammunition, rifle racks dug out of the wall, pictures from illustrated papers. But nothing really disguised the horror of these homes. You could not make space where space was not; you could not blot out the sun, nor make nectar of stewed tea, nor a Lord Mayor's banquet of army rations. You could not charm away the flies in their hosts, nor pretend you had no use for Keating's Powder. You could not dream of a bank of violets and let the breezes climb in through the loopholes.

For anywhere here one might push up the periscope and stare upon the strangest, stillest scene. It was like peering into some magic world, far, far remote from every day. One found a stretch of barren heathland, bearing such poor bushes and herbs as the pitiless sun allowed; a field of rusty browns and faded greens, and here and here brighter spots where hardy heath flowers gathered. Frail, sickly winds wandered there, causing no grass to bend its head.

Death was the farmer of that tranquil field. Look where they lie, tumbled over in every shape, all as still as still may be. Mark how the green uniforms hold the sunshine, and fail to give it back; and mark the dusky faces hideous with decay. Mark the swollen bodies. Mark the rotting eye-sockets. By night and by day shells pass over them; but ever sleep on the silent company.

We came one morning to a new post: it lay beyond our beat. The dead were thick outside and the stench sickened. A charge had swept over here the week before, up to our very rifle muzzles. Bodies lay within a few yards of the parapet. I was twisting the periscope this way and that to get a fuller view, when I picked up a fellow right before me, and so near that I was hard put to it to get the periscope down on to him. Finally I made a crack in the sandbags and looked at him face to face.

He had been crawling up, and at the last moment our man had fired point blank. In the centre of his forehead was a black hole, plain as a man might wish to see. He had made no farther movement; he had died on the moment; and now he was blackening and swelling, as the fierce suns poured over him their beams. He would swell and swell, and presently down towards the earth he would sink again, and his clothes would flap wearily whenever a wind passed by, and the rust spots would creep about his rifle. To die at the mouth of your enemy's trench—to die with your rifle at your side—a soldier may count the end a fair one, and maybe this fellow's soul had passed the gates of Paradise. And yet I must be thinking of that woman far away who cried on Allah for his safe return. I stopped up the crack in the bags, and stepped down again on to the trench floor.

Many a time one might pass this way and see never a sign of war other than men polishing rifles, nor hear a sound of it beyond the crack of a sniper at a loophole, or a thud of an enemy bullet chipping the baked parapet. You would find men shaving, and men cooking little dinners; men reading old papers and writing love letters. You would see men sleeping; and men naked to the waists, bending close over shirts, where among the seams and other crevices, with thumbnail in place of horn and hound, the hunt went forward. You might come on fatigue parties, armed with spade and sandbag, strengthening the parapet, or building new traverses, or tunnelling towards the enemy. They were all dirt and sweat and thirst, these parties; yet, the job over, there was no wash for them; they pulled on their shirts and lay back and tried to forget things in a sort of dog's doze. Grumbling was rife, and I have heard men pray for a bullet to end them, and there were mysterious accidents of a bullet through the hand or the foot, yet all the time there was heart in us. You would ever find men eager to lie of what they had done before being fool enough to join in the affair, and others ready to tell you what they were going to do when they got back. And everywhere was conviction of final victory.

The trenches were not always galleries of peace. The enemy would take evil fits and shell us. We minded this little when they sent only common shrapnel; but in course of time big guns were brought up, which was a very different matter. There was always an evening battle, for, did they leave us at peace, we were at pains to stir them up. And then there were the big attacks; but they are another story.

Other people had observing stations along here —the New Zealanders had one, and the Indian gunners one. Always we stopped for a few words in passing. The Indian men were friendly fellows. You would meet them suddenly, a white officer and two or three native telephonists. "Good day, sir." "Good day." And then Australian and Indian would salute, and we would come to a standstill.

"Anything special going on?" from the colonel.

"They're making a great work of Lonesome

Pine. They have been hard at it all the morning. Something ought to be done before it gets too strong."

Out would come the colonel's hand for the periscope. "Yes," he would say, breaking off from a long look, "Lonesome Pine and the Jolly are too strong for my liking, and too near. Something should be done right away. The places are little fortresses and stuck right under our nose." He would look again and then turn round. "I suppose you know we knocked that gun out yesterday?"

"We claim that, sir; and I hear the New Zealanders say it was theirs."

"You claim it, do you? What damned cheek! It's ours right enough. They had it out in the open; you could see the gunners standing up to it breast high. We put a shell right on top of it, and left it on its side. It's there now." He would take another long look round the landscape. "They've got a road over there; quite a thoroughfare, where mules and camels and hand-organs and such interesting things pass up and down all day. I'll give them a bit of hurry up there some time. It's quite a fashionable place, fountains and that sort of thing: probably they have afternoon tea there. A round or two would be just the thing."

"You might plug one into the band."

"Quite so. Quite so. By the way, we have been knocked down again. Five rounds per day is the limit now. I wonder why we troubled to come here? Soon we shall be told there is no more ammunition, then I shall have to throw my glasses at them, or hit them on the head with the periscope." He would continue to stare into the glass. "I think I must put a round into that road to-day. I'll do it on the way home: it will be dinner time then. They'll be out in the open, and there will be a better chance of catching somebody. Besides, it will mean a spoilt dinner, if nothing else."

They saluted, and we pushed on towards C Battery. It was on a bit of a rise called the Pimple; and a few more traverses and a few more turnings emptied us out on to it. A couple of guns were level with the trenches, and the others were a matter of two hundred yards farther back. The trench guns had good sandbagged overhead cover, and a sandbag screen before them. The country here was more open and less precipitous, and less miserable to live in, it struck me. The battery commander had built himself a good funk-hole—a square, fairly roomy place, where he passed the day when nothing important was on hand. He had much of an epicure's soul, and, being a wise man, got what good living he was able. His dishes were ever more tempting than ours. The colonel knew it, and broke his journey there on many a scorching morn. For in his heart the colonel sighed for Melbourne's fleshpots. "Yards is a poor housekeeper," I have heard him say, sadly shaking his head. Such times the major would laugh. He was stout, with a wonderful complexion, which matched the D.S.O. ribbon on his coat.

It was quiet round here, as the enemy fire passed over into the open country beyond. An entire shell missed me by feet one day, striking a bank just overhead and bursting upwards, and that was my only hurried moment in these parts.

Farther along you entered an open valley overlooking the sea. No doubt it had been scrub-covered like other hillsides, but a rest camp grew up here, and the place was all funk-holes and cook-houses and communication trenches. I don't know why the spot was chosen, as it was poorly sheltered, and at one period underwent heavy daily doses of shellfire. To reach A Battery one had to cross it and additional open country beyond. A fair road led there, taking you past a prosperous graveyard to the right hand. There were still some bushes among the graves where stayed the last of the tits and goldfinches. Later on they too flew away. The road sloped fast towards the sea, but before you had travelled far a footpath ran over the hill to meet it. This footpath came from A Battery trenches.

In early days, when the rest camp filled part of the open, you might expect one or two shells to hurry you on the way. It might happen there would be more than one or two. On a certain hazy morning the colonel and I came back from A Battery. We reached the end of the footpath where it finished on the road. The shrapnel was falling down the valley in generous style and here and here, without plan. The rest camp had gone to ground, and such unlucky fellows as were abroad on business spent as short time on their errands as possible. The colonel sat down on the bank to cool and allow the Turkish gunners to tire; but five minutes went by and matters were unaltered. Then he stood again, to look keenly up the valley towards the C Battery funk-holes, the while humping his shoulders and stroking his nose with the periscope. "Lake!" he cried out of a sudden in his quick way, "it's Kismet!" And we ran.

A Battery fellows were to be envied; their views were the finest anywhere about. They had a broad blue view of the sea, and they could gaze their fill on impregnable Achi-Baba. Some mornings no wrinkle aged the hot waters; and the fleets were all asleep. Other mornings the battleships stood off Achi-Baba, hurling vast shells on to the ridges. You could hear the rumbling, and could watch the cones of dust rise into the skies. But fire as the sailors might, the army beyond the hills never drew more near.

The A Battery men could see Gaba Tepeh down below, and not far away either. It ran into the sea like a cigar or a man's finger. One might watch the ruined observing station, and guess at the wire entanglements. From a wide ledge outside the first communication trench was the best view of all. From there one morning the colonel and I sighted the *Albion* aground. She had run over a mudbank in a submarine scare. Gaba Tepeh peppered away with might and main, and a battleship in the straits—the *Goeben* they said—tossed great shells across the Peninsula. Round the unhappy boat fussed the *Canopus*, trying what hawsers might do. Our watch ended as finally the *Albion* slipped away. "There she goes!" burst out the colonel, shutting up his glasses. "There she scuttles away like a ——!" No, I had better not.

Already I have told you of the flat country dividing us from Achi-Baba. In the haze of sunshine hours it was revealed rich, cultivated, and broken by trees. It was a home for shepherdesses and lovesick, piping shepherds. But it was false as it was fair.

For in an olive grove towards the farther side there lurked a gun named Beachy Bill. By day and by night he waited there, preying upon the beach and the anchorage. Incredible bags stood to his account, and my own back was grazed by his pellet on an unlucky afternoon. Would that I could boast as Beachy Bill!

He had a comrade—a warrior after his heart—the Anafarta gun. This comrade fired from Anafarta, the low land beyond our left, and one or other would sweep the beach all hours of the day. Did you leave the shelter of the provision stacks, you took life in your hands. They would snipe at the crowds at the water tanks, and at the bathers in the sea. They would send the sandbags flying into the dug-outs, and scatter the cheeses and the biscuit cases. They were the scourge of all who dwelt upon the beach. Aye, would that I had proved myself as well!

In spite of the pastoral outlook, A Battery had few peaceful hours. The enemy judged their whereabouts with accuracy, and half a dozen shells tore over directly they opened their mouths. Through the long summer many stretchers made the journey to the beach. And the gunners left behind grew browner and leaner, and swore more heartfelt oaths.

CHAPTER XVI

A FLAG OF TRUCE

EVERY afternoon, at four o'clock sometimes, sometimes at five o'clock, sometimes later even, we had our evening battle. The morning rounds completed, the colonel returned to Headquarters, where I saw no more of him for an hour or two. That time was my own, when I crawled under the wretched awning of my funk-hole, and settled down to grill through the heat of the day. By three or four o'clock invariably the colonel came to life again, arriving in the open to stretch and collect periscope and glasses. Then he would call out, "Come on, Lake!" and tread again the little path up the hill to the valley head.

Sometimes we took the left-hand trenches, where there was an observing station in Sands's charge; but more often at the B Battery observing station the fight had birth.

Every evening we asked for trouble, put in a round here and a round there until we got it, and with little enough need it seemed; but maybe the army would have lost hope had nothing like this happened. For through much of the day—when even the flies fell exhausted into the tea—

the snipers of either army lost heart to snipe, and the gunners lay by their guns wondering how it was they could not die. But as the sun climbed down his ladder, and a flagging breeze puffed off the sea, we rose again to our feet, picked up periscopes and telephones, and goaded ourselves into another evening hate.

At this time—late spring or early summer—the Turkish army had lately spent a mighty effort to drive us into the sea. Purging the beach of our presence, they called it in their newspapers. The old knowledge was reproven—hopeless to attack well-armed, well-entrenched troops. At the end of several fierce hours the attempt was spent, and the enemy reeled to his trenches leaving on a few acres of ground between three and four thousand dead. Everywhere you looked the dead men lay, and hours later you might see an arm move or a leg rise, where some poor fellow cried on Death not to delay. In time the breath of decay searched you out the length of Shrapnel Valley, and when the wind veered in the trenches it caught you by the throat. I marvelled how the men there got down their dinners.

One evening, on the heels of the big attack, we had a pretty little battle. The colonel observed from B Battery station, and I carried orders to the telephonist a few yards away.

The major had not turned up, and Mr. Hay was in charge. B Battery was dusting up "C" or "Collins Street" or one of the usual targets, and the other batteries banged away elsewhere with more than daily hate. A great many snipers were at work too on either side. We had woken up this afternoon.

The great heat of the day had passed, indeed there were one or two signs of evening. The sun was three parts of the way down the sky, and shadows started to grow at the bottom of every bush. The high noon haze was no more, and you could see with great clearness over all the desolate country. Our shells burst in sudden white clouds on the great hill in the distance; and here and here, did you know where to look, moved the puff of the enemy's return fire. And nearer at hand, you could follow the Turkish trenches by the vicious, short-lived dust spurts of our bullets.

Where the colonel took his stand, they were tunnelling out a machine-gun position; and every few moments men came out of the earth with freshly filled sandbags on their shoulders. They crowded the narrow passage, blocking me every time I hurried to Mr. Hay or the telephonist.

The colonel stood on a platform, head just under the parapet, periscope just above. His size caused him to crouch, and his legs were wide apart. The brisker grew the battle, the more engrossed became he; so that now he never moved his head, but stayed bent forward staring into the glass. His exclamations made to himself were to be heard. "That's a good one! Very good! Right on the target! That's pretty shooting! Green's into 'em now! Oh, damn! now they're off! Hay has got off! Are you there, Lake?"

I stood just below watching for the least sign, for when he grew interested, often a movement of the hand was all his signal, and at best he would jerk out an abrupt word or two. Now I answered, "Yes, sir," and stood ready. "Tell Mr. Hay to come over more. Two degrees more right. That's better, that's better! Still he can come over more. Two degrees more right, tell him!"

Away went I. Mr. Hay was at the periscope and nodded to show he had heard. As I moved off again, he called out: "Tell the colonel they seem to be waving flags over there. They seem to want to attract attention. They were doing it before, and now they have started again." I told the colonel what he said, but got no answer for my pains. I would have looked myself had there been time.

"That's better, that's better!" the colonel started to say. "Now he is short! Damn it, he's short! Lake, tell him to add fifty. Say he wants fifty or a hundred." I took the message and came back again, finding time to sit down. The action went on, losing little or nothing of its briskness. Then came word down the line, passed in a mysterious unofficial way, that something was happening on the other side; the enemy was waving flags and looking over the parapets, as if to attract attention. But it seemed no more was to come of it, as the fire went on and the moment's excitement was spent. Yet five minutes later it had grown again, and methought something must happen now. I itched to see how matters went, but I must not leave the spot. The firing lost heart, becoming a number of sharp explosions in place of an unbroken roll. Again the word came along. The colonel took interest finally and stopped a passing officer to inquire, and next looked again at the opposite trenches. Finally he gave word for the batteries to cease fire, and stepped down on to the floor of the trench. Our part in the battle was over. I lost no time picking up a periscope and seeing all there was to see. It was little enough worth the bother. The enemy must have given up their idea, for not one flag flew, gaze as I would. I soon tired and sat down on a ledge belonging to some machine gunners who lived round here. It was their habit to sleep through the day and come out at evening. Each man had a recess of his own, with a blanket hung before it to cheat the sun. Their legs only were left in sight. It came about that I knew them better by their feet than their faces.

When I sat down, the colonel disappeared. Maybe he went to pass the time of day with an infantry colonel whose dug-out was a few steps down the path. Commonly he did this, leaving me in the trench to call him if need be. Just now were several sets of legs showing beyond the blankets, and a half-hearted argument went forward.

"I joined fer the six bob of course: what else'd a bloke do it fer?"

"I joined 'cos I 'ad a row with the old woman. I went out in a 'urry and joined right away, and I blasted well wish I 'adn't."

"What did you join fer, Darkie? Was it the six bob, or a row with yer tart, or was the police after yer?" Darkie made no answer. "Wot was it, Darkie?"

"I joined cos I thought a bloke ought ter join."

It was like the bursting of an 8·25 shell. Nobody said anything. Nobody moved at all. I looked around for a museum to put the sentiment in.

We were wide awake this afternoon, and a brisk musketry fire continued. I sat where I was, hearing the noise and yet not hearing it. The sun had stepped another rung down his ladder, a few shadows spread about, and there was even a suggestion of evening cool. I don't know what I thought of, nothing probably, for the place had power to destroy one mentally and morally. Then without warning there woke again the former interest. "They're waving the flags," came down from the right. "There's something doing! There's something up!"

I got up with a yawn and went to the parapet, and there poked up the periscope, and interest came with a vengeance. Straight before me was a big white flag charged with a red crescent, moving slowly forwards and backwards over the enemy parapet, and while I watched a second one rose up on our right and at odd intervals appeared other streamers which might have been small flags and might have been rags. Round me all who by hook or by crook could get hold of a periscope were on the platforms finding out what was happening, and this must have taken place over a great deal of the line, as presently the musketry became completely broken up and on the point of cessation.

I had taken stand among the B Battery men, beside their periscope, where the parapet was quite low, and it wanted no effort to look over the top. I fell to debating whether to take the risk and see first hand how matters went, and while yet I stayed uncertain something happened to decide me on the moment. There was a movement in the enemy's trench beside the largest flag, and a man climbed over the parapet and dropped on to the open ground. He stood still a moment in uneasy fashion, next took into his hands the big white flag with the red crescent, held it overhead, and came forward. I felt like crying out my admiration. Our snipers shot yet in scores, in hundreds may be; and any moment a stray shot or the aimed shot of a fool might tumble him over where he stood. And no one knew the danger better than himself, for he bowed his head and upper body as does a man advancing in the teeth of a great wind, and came forward with deliberate steps, moving his wide flag in wider semicircles. To the devil with caution, said I, and stood right up and looked across the open. "By Jove!" I must exclaim out loud. "By Jove!" Beside me was Mr. Hay, and he looked round to know had I gone mad.

News had travelled everywhere that something special was on hand, for cries went up and down: "Cease fire there! Cease fire!" And the firing did die away, though unwillingly, lessening and returning again in gusts, like an April wind or a woman's last word in an argument. Even when you might say the musketry had stopped, there was still a splutter and a cracking here and here, for there are ever fools who cannot help themselves.

But all this while the man of peace continued on his way, at the same stride and in the same bent attitude. May be ere starting on the journey he had delivered his soul into Allah's safekeeping, for no shot touched him, and no quick fear turned him from the path. There was something that moved me deep down as I looked on his unhurried pace and the slow waving of his flag. It plucked my heart strings to see him alone there, his life not worth a smoked-out cigarette. I stood right up, all my upper body above the parapet, so that the countryside was bared before me, and a draught of evening wind born of wide spaces came a-knocking at my nostrils. All my heart cried out to him. "My salute, friend, my salute! Do you hear me over there? It is Gunner Lake who calls. A brave man's heart is crying out to a brave man! My salute, friend! In all honour I offer my salute!"

When the man of peace had advanced halfway, the musketry fire of both sides was nearly silent, and there was a stir of uncertainty in our ranks. You heard some crying, "Cease fire," and others calling out against it, shouting there was no order, and what the devil was everyone about. But the firing did not start again, or only in short-lived bursts, and the men hung by the loopholes, waiting what might befall. There was a stir on our side now, near Clayton's trench it seemed from here, and soon an officer came into the open, with a handkerchief tied on to a stick or a rifle, I did not notice which. At the same time a couple of Turks hopped from their trenches, and another of our men went forward; and it seemed they would hold a parley then and there. While I looked to see, I found the colonel at my shoulder.

"Get the interpreter, Lake," he said quickly. "Get Bargi and bring him here. He may be wanted." Over I went to the telephonist and sent down word, then back again I came and told the colonel, and next up I jumped once more to look over the country.

The little company had come together and were in parley. The distance was a matter of hundreds of yards, so there was little enough to see and nothing to be heard. I hoped when Bargi came the colonel would go over there, and I grew eager for his coming. I had become impatient, and cursed him for his fatness, when a second big flag was put up to our right hand, and two men jumped into the open and came towards our trenches, one empty-handed and one bearing with him the standard. The colonel looked round sharply, and made as if to go over there, then of a sudden he turned to me.

"Where's Bargi, Lake? Where's Bargi?"

"He's on the way, sir."

"Meet him and hurry him up. Say I want him at once!"

I pushed towards the trench mouth as speedily as could be managed, not the least eager for the run down the hill and back again. But at the turn I met Bargi blowing with his exertions, and a look half-pleased, half-scared, on his sweating face. He was a little Italian Jew who spoke and wrote a dozen languages. By trade he had been art photographer, traveller for a firm of jewellers, and one or two other things as best I could make out. War was declared, times grew hard, and he made up his mind to go a-soldiering. But he mistook his trade. He was the most cowardly man in the brigade. "My disposition is very nervous," he said to me once. "I am too sensitive." And he shrugged his shoulders deprecatingly. "Sensitive," thought I. "Good friend, we call it by another name."

He got on badly with the other men, and I was sorry for him, and on the whole liked him well enough. Now I pulled him up, and he panted and asked what was wanted. "The colonel wants you in a hurry. He is waiting a few yards up the trench." No more was said. Bargi went on without more speech, and I turned to follow. But Lewis pulled at my sleeve and asked what was happening. He had been Bargi's guide up here. "There's a bit of an armistice on," I called out as I turned. "Have a look for yourself. I have to get after the colonel." And with no more I left Lewis standing in the middle of the path, his hands in his pockets, and a silly stare on his face. Lewis may have been a pretty fellow to look at; but he was a rank bore.

The couple of seconds' delay had lost me Bargi; and I did my best to catch him before he met the colonel and both disappeared. Fortune nodding, I saw their heels rounding a traverse, and caught up with them quite soon. The trench was rather empty, and the colonel moved in a great hurry, so that fat little Bargi, who had not found breath, was hard put to it to keep up. We dodged round one turning and then another, nobody speaking all the way. Sometimes Bargi threw timid glances over a shoulder at me, for it was his first trench journey, and truly he was receiving a brusque introduction. Presently the press of men grew again, curbing us to a slower rate; and next we met a crossway, which brought us to a standstill. Someone put us on to the right road, and we started anew to elbow forward. Finally we found our way into a sap, and this ending, we had come as far as was possible. The colonel put up his periscope to find where we were, and I jumped up on to a platform and poked my head over the parapet. You could hear the crack of a rifle now and again, but not often.

We had come to the best spot. The men and the flag were opposite. They were nearer than before, yet they had not come far over, and at this moment still looked before them in an undecided fashion. I do not doubt they cared little for the exposed position. Almost at once Bargi climbed up beside me, and there were the three of us in a row—the colonel looking into the periscope, the Jew standing on tip-toe, peeping over the parapet, and throwing away no chance of protection, and myself at the end of the line. The two Turks continued to delay, in fact went so far as to make a motion of retreat. "Call them, Bargi!" the colonel burst out. "Tell them to come on; say it's all right!"

The little man looked anxiously about, but pulled himself together and called out something in Turkish. His words failed to carry all the way, so that he clapped hands to his mouth and cried out anew, this time at the top of his voice. At once the Turks were reassured; they scanned eagerly to find the voice, and after exchange of a sentence or two, came forward deliberately, the man with the standard bearing it high above his head. They were entering our half of the debatable country when some fool to the right hand fired, and set a dozen others pulling triggers. The Turks turned about, and made for home at a shambling trot; but with the speed of birth the fire died, and the peacemakers steadied their retreat. Then Bargi called again, in time to reassure, for the runners doubtfully came back, the standard-bearer holding his flag at top height. They drew quite near, near enough for me to see clearly their appearance, when it was plainly discovered they were men of different rank.

The standard-bearer was a cut-throat-looking fellow with a black moustache and a complexion scarce lighter. I doubt if he were a pure-bred Turk. He was small and well shaped; but there was that in his expression which made me fear for any dog of an unbeliever who might pass his way. He was dressed in the green uniform, with their strange pleated cap on his head. Through all the dealings he spoke no word.

The man beside him, the empty-handed man, was quite otherwise. He was dressed as an officer, and proved a doctor. He was a man of manners, a man of civilisation, a gentleman. He came to the parley with French on his lips.

The two men crossed the half-line boundary, and came so close in that the colonel put up his hand to stop them, lest they should arrive on top of our works. "Tell them to stay there, Bargi!" he broke out. "Tell them to come no farther!" Bargi halted them. He had taken courage, the fire being dead; he spoke fluently, and seemed to enjoy his importance. His dusky face glowed with satisfaction and sweat.

"Get up, Bargi," the colonel said of a sudden. "Go out and meet them. It's quite safe, man. Go on!"

Poor little Bargi collapsed. It was one matter to peep over a parapet top, and quite another to stand up in the open like a tree, a target for all the world. He gave the colonel a look of agony. "Hurry up, man!" was what he got for his trouble.

He began his climb, and I had scrambled up first and pulled him the last of the way. He made no attempt to go farther, and it did not matter, the Turks having arrived within talking distance. Yet it seemed fate would refuse us our parley, for someone let a machine gun loose —Australian or Turk I do not know, but may Allah smite him! The bullets sang by my head like a swarm of mad bees. There was no time for "After you, sir." Bargi tumbled back into the trench, and I jumped down on top of him. A brisk burst of rifle fire broke out on both sides, and then died with all suddenness. Next I was up on the parapet again. The Turkish peace-makers had run for their own lines, for now they returned.

Bargi was sadly disinclined for a second re-appearance in the open, but there was nothing for it, and presently he stood on top beside me. The Turks were near at hand again, too close for the colonel's pleasure; and he waved Bargi forward in abrupt fashion. Openly reluctant, Bargi went.

The meeting was a meeting of dancing masters. They put their hands to their foreheads and bowed profoundly; they advanced and bowed once more; they smiled with utmost courtesy and bowed anew. Next they fell to talking loudly, but in the accents of men who ask the other's good health, and who rejoice at the fine-ness of the day. And while they talked, I picked out a seat on the mound before the parapet, and sat down to watch. It was so near evening one might sit at ease out in the sunlight.

Aye, it was a sight you might seek in vain on many a summer's day. There stood up the two great armies, the Turkish army and the troops of Australasia, filling the mouths of the trenches, and staring one another in the face. Men that had lived days on end between two narrow, sun-baked walls, men that had lifted heads above a certain level at risk of their lives, now looked over the great bare country, and widened their lungs with breezes new from the sea. The sky was filling with clear white clouds, the ground was sown with shadows; and endless heights and depths climbed up and tumbled away. And there were swift greens and blues and greys splashed over the picture, and earthy reds, and glistening patches of sand. And for background were the big hills leaning against the sky.

And rank after rank, from foot to skyline, stood soldiers in their thousands. The reserves were countless. And look you to the right hand, and look you to the left, you were met by our men, their heads lifted over the parapets, or themselves a-top swinging their legs. And between the armies lay the debatable land, pocked with dead men and broken rifles. Ye gods! it was a sight worth the looking.

Where I sat the ground fell sharply away, and a few yards down the slope rested three of our dead, lying with heads close together. And look where you would, you would come on part of a man—a pair of boots pushed from a mound; a hand; an elbow; or may be it was the flutter of a piece of coat. The burials had been by night—graves forced from hard ground, with few minutes to give to the building. The mounds had settled and betrayed their secrets.

Of Turks fallen in the last attack there was no end: it was a day's task to count them.

There came down the line word that General Runner parleyed with the other group. I looked across. Several men stood together, but no more could I discover.

No sooner was the fire of both armies well dead than a number of Turks jumped from their trenches and fell with right good energy to filling their arms with the rifles which lay in scores about the field. Speedily men were staggering home loaded to their limit. And a sniper who sniped from an exposed position fell to digging himself in in generous style. The colonel let out a bellow. "Stop those men! Stop them this minute! Bargi, stop those men!" Bargi grasped what was wanted, pointed it out to the flag-bearers, and with lusty shouting the men were recalled. But the manœuvre gained the enemy half a hundred rifles; and methinks the sniper had a more spacious parlour from that hour.

It was our last interruption. It seemed the enemy asked a truce for the burial of their dead. Bargi ran forwards and backwards, swollen with importance. The colonel could do no more than receive the message; but the brigadier was with the other group and would have more power. In course of time word arrived empowering the colonel to announce the enemy might send a staff officer by way of Gaba Tepeh next morning, when the matter would be discussed. Bargi floundered over the explanation, and a big lieutenant of infantry climbed up to help him. The man must have been among the largest in the army. "You'll be a good advertisement for Australia," the colonel said. And seeing I was all anxiety to follow, he added, "No, Lake, this is not your stunt."

It was all over presently. The men of truce

agreed to take back the message, and fire would open again in a few minutes. Afresh they saluted, afresh they bowed: and our men came this way, and they turned that. The colonel gathered up glasses and periscope; and we went off to tea. On the way we ran into a party placing in position a trench mortar. And farther on we met men hurrying up with ammunition. We had roared at the Turkish treachery; but who shall say our honour was over-nice? As I sat at tea, the firing broke out again in a great roll.

Their staff officer rode into our lines next morning. He reappeared the morning after also, and the outcome was a truce of half a day. Certain rules were framed. Parties of so many from either side were allowed over so many yards, and neither party might penetrate beyond half-way. We would take their dead to them, and they would bring our dead to us.

The day and the hour came round, and peace fell over the armies. The silence was very strange. About the middle of the morning the colonel set off as usual for the trenches, and we started the rounds as on any other day from the B Battery observing station. No shot was to be heard, and the trenches were emptier of men than I had seen them. Without delay we passed to C Battery on the Pimple, and there joined Colonel Irons, Major Andrews, and Major Green.

Behind C Battery and before A, the five of us climbed from the trenches on to open ground. The sun was out, but the day was cool; and it was pleasant to stand up at ease in the open. A great gathering had come about on the debatable land. It was like a day at the races, with a shabby crowd in attendance. The rule limiting the number of parties was slackly enforced, and anyone tying a white bandage to his arm to denote stretcher-bearer could go where he wanted. In this way there were numbers exploring on their own account, exchanging mementoes with the enemy, and seeing what was to be seen. The camera fiend was at large.

The burial of the dead went forward in harmony if not in love. Our fellows were good willed enough and eager with curiosity; but among the enemy were many glum countenances. Nor do I wonder, for it is but chilly amusement gazing into the faces of your own dead.

There were many strange sights to be found in a few hundred yards' marching; but I have not time to tell a tenth of them. At one place was a crater in the ground where a shell had burst; and round it, like chickens come to feed at a basin, lay eight dead men. It was the prettiest bit of shooting that you might wish to see. And not so very far away was a gully, maybe twenty yards long, half that wide, and half again that deep. The Turkish stretcher-bearers had gathered dead from everywhere, and tumbled them here—the place was a-choke with bodies. Hundreds were there. They lay a dozen deep. They made me catch my breath. But it was when we turned to go over to A Battery that we passed the scene it will take me longest to forget.

Four of our own fellows lay on their backs in

the grass, all within a few paces. They were of those who had fallen in the first rush, and had been overlooked. Their clothes were little stained, for no rains had touched them, and their hats were still cocked to one side in the jauntiest manner.

The first man was a skeleton, picked as clean as a century of waiting might do. His skull looked out between the tunic and the hat; and through the bones of his hands grasses had woven a road. One could only gape at the fellow.

The next man waited on his back too; but the fierce suns had done otherwise with him. The flesh had decayed under the skin, while the skin had stayed, becoming a dark parchment drawn tightly over the bones. Every hair on head and hand remained. Face and hands were tiny, the face and hands of a child they were: yet the face was full of expression, and more terrible to look on than the face of any ape.

The third man was as the second.

The fourth man had swollen up and afterwards sunk down again. I had to turn away and spit.

And those four men had been filled with great foolish hopes but a few weeks before. Amen! Amen!

Come, hang up the gun by the chimney!
Come, scabbard the sword and the dirk!
And we'll tip-toe afar,
Where the sunbeams still are,
Leaving spider and mouse to their work.
The moon yet doth ride through the night, friend,
The sun yet doth warden the day:
And we'll lie down and rest,
On the earth's ample breast,
While these rivers of blood run away.

Come, loosen the belt and the tunic,
Uncover your head from its steel!
Leave the mess-tin to rust!
Let the flask choke with dust!
There are better things needing our zeal.
The harvest is heavy with waiting,
The eyes of our women are red;
Then stay but an hour,
While the hills break in flower,
And the grasses climb over our dead!

Oh foolish, oh foolish this striving!
Oh empty this passion and hate!
I am laboured of breath:
I am weary to death:
Come, let us forgive ere too late!
Come, lend me your hand for a space, friend!
The hours and the minutes race by!
But we've time to lie back
On the side of the track,
Till these channels of blood have run dry.

CHAPTER XVII

THE MARCH OF MONOTONY

The weeks marched by, one upon the heels of the next; and summer came down upon that cruel land. All day long the suns stared at the baked ground, and the flies multiplied beyond imagination. The enemy, sitting in the opposite trenches, was less terrible than this pitiless season. There was no savour in the food; the water ration could not quench the thirst; there was no new scene on which to feed the eye; there was no change of duty. We were no step nearer the end of affairs. And typhus and dysentery began to stalk abroad. A man had but to keep his mouth shut to prove his heroism.

Between the attacks, the fellows sat or lay all day long in a sort of dog's doze. Frequently they had put up awnings of waterproof sheets; but the heat below was close and sickly. Fellows were bare legged and stripped naked to the waist, with big patches of broken skin where the sun had blistered. And there were men burnt as brown as niggers. Here and here were groups smoking, playing cards, and talking. I heard little said of the war, which had long since failed to interest; but there were endless stories of race-horses and prize-fighters, and endless boasts about girls. And many liars told and retold their most brilliant lies. Thus crawled by the fiery hours between rise and set of sun.

Little Billy Blake meets me in the valley one mid-day. "Have you heard about poor Bill Eaves?" he says. "What's up?" say I. "Dead," he says. "Damned sorry to hear that," say I. "How did it happen?" "Don't know. They found him at the top of the valley. A shrapnel bullet had copped him in the top of the napper. I helped to take him down to the beach. 'Struth, I was sweating at the end!" "Bad luck for old Bill," say I. "Blasted bad luck," says he. "So long," say I. "So long," says he. And he goes on down the valley; and I climb up the hill to headquarters.

Sooner or later you met all the celebrities poking round in the trenches. Once General Rivers came daily to the Pimple, smoking a cigarette in a long thin holder. He had a favourite seat beside one of C Battery guns. He was tall and thin, with a slight stoop as I remember, and an air of great refinement for a soldier. His hands were white, with long fingers, and nails so clean he might have walked off the Collins Street Block. He sat and smoked silently, or walked up and down, pointing quietly with his hand. I don't know how he treated his Staff; but he seemed reasonable in his dealings.

Another man with the face of a student was Captain Carrot, the war correspondent. I took him about the trenches more than once. He was rather tall and rather thin, with a peaky face and glasses. He carried a camera in place of a rifle. In Egypt he had written an article which had much offended the army; and many were the threats against him. But someone told me, in a charge down Cape Helles way, he had exposed himself to get a good view, and so he was forgiven. I don't know how true is the story; but his popularity came back. He had little to say to me.

A third man frequently run to earth in the trenches was Colonel Saxon, V.C. He was a quiet man with a polished manner and a lisp. I heard he came from a crack English regiment. He left his staff behind him, and poked about on his own account, periscope under arm, and nothing more. He was never put out; he took all as a part of a day's happenings, even the shortage of men and ammunition, and the brigadier's wrath. "The general is awfully angry with me this morning," he lisped to the colonel once when we ran into him. "I don't know what I've done. I thought I had better go for a walk while he cools down. Everything is quite dead to-day. I'm off now by Quinn's Post. Good-bye."

And last—and very far from least—on some fine mornings round the corner strolled General Birdwood, with his A.D.C., his periscope bearer, his mapcase bearer, and all the following of a mighty man of war. He was a popular general. As often as not his dress was a sun helmet, a plain khaki shirt, corduroy knickerbockers, and leggings cut after the style of an English squire or well-to-do yeoman. He carried a walking-stick in his hand. In his ways he was calm and easy going. His face showed good temper; but there was a chin at the bottom of it; and he looked the manner of man who would haul off and lay you out rather than put you under arrest. He spoke to all and sundry in the trenches, and bathed freely with the men in the sea. I stood beside him once when he had a squeak from a sniper. The bullet chipped down the earth on us. "Now, where's that rascal?" the general said, lifting up his head. "Can't any of you men get rid of him? We ought not to allow that." One or other of his A.D.C.'s followed at his heels; and it might be brigadiers and lesser fry swelled the train, until one had to push against the trench wall to let the procession go by.

As summer wore on, and the fighting slackened away to daily skirmishes, there came much talk of reinforcements of men and guns, and a second attempt to carry the Peninsula by storm. There was much talk, I say; but there was nothing more. The endless suns baked the earth to brick, and parched in men's hearts the seeds of hope. The stretchers took their loads down to the beach; and it was a trench won here and a trench lost there, that was all. But one looked in vain for the transports steaming East.

The colonel kept to his habits all the time: we tramped up and down hill in the morning, and in the evening we had our battle. Once he went away for a change, and came back with his old energy. The sun peeled the skin from the end of his nose, and burnt his face a fierce red; his clothes began to wear, and he changed them for a private's issue, so that a great deal of his glory departed. But his keenness stayed after his beauty had faded.

Our targets changed little. It might be the enemy brought up a new battery or retired an old one: and steadily they strengthened their trenches and sapped towards us, as we on our own account sapped towards them. They made two fortresses of Lonesome Pine and Jackson's Jolly; and ever at sight of those the colonel wagged his head and was full of misgiving. The Jolly was named after him on account of his fears of it, and I believe he christened Lonesome Pine. From our side Lonesome Pine was no more than a sandbagged mound, with a small blasted sapling standing up at one point. The sapling was of no appearance; but in that bare country it made a landmark. It was strange the enemy allowed it to stay. The colonel pointed it out to a friend. "They're doing an awful lot of work over there," says he. "Right in our mouth," says he. "You see where I mean, that mound with the stick on it. It reminds you of that book—what's it, *The Trail of the Lonesome Pine* or something." The other man looks hard at it and shakes his head, and then they fall to talking on another subject. Says the other man, "You had a gun blown out yesterday, didn't you?" "I think it can be fixed up," says the colonel. "Three men went with it." And then he wags his head with very great sadness. "You can get new guns; but you can't send down to Hell for new gunners."

There would be days when the sun was less terrible, and sea and sky were calm with the wonderful blue calm of the Mediterranean. Then the open country between us and Achi-Baba became a forbidden Eden. I forget how often the colonel and I have stared at it covered with the sleepy sunshine. "Look at it, look at it," he would mutter. "What a place for love and fishing!"

Towards evening the D battalion officers congregated at the top of Shrapnel Valley by a curtained dug-out used as an office. They drifted there in ones and twos to smoke and yawn and stare at the sea. From here you looked down the length of Shrapnel Valley on camps clustering all the way. The signallers wagged to one another to keep in practice, and the reinforcements drilled on a flat open space at the lower end. A few shells might be travelling forwards and backwards, but frequently there was no more sound than the lazy crack of the snipers. Overlooking this, the D Battalion officers sat on up-ended packing cases and smoked. And with them often sat the colonel, and not far off I leaned against the bank, exchanging news with the telephonists in the office. "Who would think this was war?" says the colonel, rubbing his nose with the end of the periscope. "Half a dozen men sitting on boxes smoking and cursing the flies. And a beautiful blue sea to look at, and a beautiful blue sky overhead. I always pictured myself galloping into action at the head of my brigade and flourishing a sword. Why a sword I don't know; but it was like a picture in a story book, and there were red bombs bursting round my head. And now I have to tramp up and down these dirty hills. I won't come again. I shall send someone else instead. Did you see what Hamilton said in brigade orders—'the incomparable Twenty-ninth.' That rather blows us out, doesn't it? You can't easily beat 'incomparable.' I suppose when a general hasn't had his name in the paper for a few days, he starts writing 'incomparable' and 'glorious' and 'magnificent' before his troops; and then the people at home say, 'Those men have been through a hard time. That general must be a hell of a clever fellow.'"

Truly one might look down this valley and not think of war. There were no armed men about, and many fellows wore flannel shirts open at the neck, and knickerbockers cut above the knee, and legs bare the rest of the way, so that little was to show of the original uniform. Roads worn solid by passage of many feet led to the principal places, and the thick scrub that once had made this valley so difficult and so romantic had long gone as firewood for the cooks. I have seen mining camps with all the same appearance. But in time the secret was given away. It might be the enemy sent us half a dozen big shells at tea-time, or on the way up or down you passed a stretcher making the journey to the beach.

Once I met a dead man lying on the side of the road. His lower body was naked and mottled, and the two legs stuck stiffly into the air with toes apart. I saw nobody attending to him, though he was gone when I came back. Another day there came a great burst of clapping from the lower part of the valley, so that fellows left their work and turned about to know what went forward. Presently news hurried along that the war was over, as the Kaiser had murdered the Crown Prince; but later I heard the peaceful morning had tempted from his funk-hole a well-known dug-out king. Hence the applause.

We met a little man one tea-time just below Infantry Headquarters. We came down from our evening battle, and he was striding up. "Good day, sir," he says, and salutes. "Hallo, captain," cries the colonel. "I thought you were down at Helles?" "Back again," says the captain. "You had a hot time down there," says the colonel. "Pretty hot," says the captain; "ha! ha! It was their machine guns that played the deuce. Ha, ha, ha! You know, two or three men with machine guns can hold up a battalion. Ha, ha! You know, before very long war will be one man in an armoured box, turning a treadle, ha ha! and setting fifty machine guns going. Ha, ha! Ha, ha, ha!" "Well, so long, I'm off to tea," says the colonel. And away we go.

The bitter monotony of every day put men at their wit's end to escape the place, and fellows went sick unaccountably, and had strange bullet wounds in hand or foot. And this brings to mind a man I met near Clayton's trenches. The enemy was giving us hurry-up with five- and six-inch shells, and the colonel led the way in solid style by back trenches towards E Battery observing station. The shells arrived one or two per minute, and burst with a dull roar. Some fell ahead of us and some behind us, and there was no reason one should not fall atop of us. Therefore, as we had no call here, it was prudent to choose a healthier locality. At a traverse corner a parapet had come down, and a man stood trapped by the legs, pulling to and fro to get free. I fell on my knees to drag away the dirt. Soon I had loosed him so that his efforts did the rest. He came free, panting and rather scared; but in no manner hurt it seemed. I jumped up again, and the colonel, who waited near by, set the pace anew. I had forgotten all about him by tea-time, when I met a procession going down to the beach. The centre figure was the hero of the afternoon, and a man supported him on either side. A third man carried his equipment, and a fourth his pack and blankets. "Off for a holiday," thought I. "Well, here's luck."

The *Triumph*, who had laboured long and hard in our cause, was torpedoed in sight of the army. We came out of the trenches upon a group of officers and men staring to sea with glasses to their eyes. They were tongue-tied, except for one or two murmurs of regret. Not far off Gaba Tepeh lay the battleship listing to one side: to her aid raced destroyers from all over the bay. They closed about her and began the work of rescue; and Gaba Tepeh seized the opportunity of a lifetime, and opened fiercely with shrapnel. The destroyers blazed back, the flashes winked like Morse lights; and a brisk engagement followed. The work of rescue went forward, and presently the *Triumph* heeled over with increasing speed, and next with a plunge she disappeared—disappeared but for her red keel, which floated for some while. The destroyers remained to pick up survivors, and next they dispersed. Gaba Tepeh shut her mouth. And we men who watched from the hilltop put away our glasses and looked at one another. There was a great muttering and shaking of heads. "Damned bad. Damned bad!" This was the first warning submarines had come so far abroad, and the navy took fright and steamed away. In time remained only destroyers and such light craft. There followed submarine scares, and hunts were organised, when aeroplanes patrolled the bay and destroyers followed. The hunt might continue all day, but I never heard of a capture.

The aeroplanes of both armies grew bold, so that our men sailed over the enemy trenches to observe and bomb, and the enemy treated us to like programme, usually at tea-time. Yards, the adjutant, went up sometimes, and the colonel would crane his neck and watch him. Says the colonel one day: "I shall not try and fly until I become an angel. I'm a nervous little fellow." The enemy planes were German Taubes, which circled overhead in fashion most trying to those below. When the bomb came free, it sounded as if it fell in a succession of dives, and gave no hint of its target. Then came the final rush, and a moment of fierce suspense; and then the roar of the bursting bomb. And then may be went abroad the cry for stretcher-bearers.

With such diversions as I tell of, the summer wore on.

CHAPTER XVIII

REALITIES

I HAD finished breakfast half an hour, and now loafed by my funk-hole while the colonel shaved. The corporal came over to me, dirty and very tired. He looked at me, head on one side, until I wondered what he wanted. At last he said: "Have you heard about Lewis?"

"What about Lewis?" I answered.

"Had his head blown off this morning."

"My God!" I said. We looked at each other a little while. "How did it happen?"

"He was Sands's telephonist first shift. When Sands got to the other end there was no sign of Lewis, and I was told to ask about him on my road. An infantry bloke said there was a dead artilleryman round the corner. I found Lewis there all right, covered with a sack. Half his head's blown off." The corporal felt his chin, which badly wanted a shave.

"Damned bad luck for poor Lewis," I said, after a silence. And what more was there to say? The corporal shrugged his shoulders, lingered a moment, and went off to his dug-out.

I sat down on the ground to wait for the colonel.

It was early yet; but already the sun menaced us. It was the start of another heartbreaking day. The flies in their tens of thousands blackened every shady place, and made ready to drowse and drone through the noon. For the thousandth time since breakfast, I brushed them from my lips. While I sat there with drooped head, thinking a little of Lewis and a good deal of nothing at all, Sands climbed down the path towards me. I got up.

"Lake, the colonel won't want you this morning. You are to wait here for Bombardier Norris and the stretcher, and guide him to Lewis. You know where Lewis is: in the communication trench leading to Clayton's. Afterwards you can go on to the B Battery observing station. The colonel is going that way."

I answered, "Yes, sir," and he said nothing more, yet he did not go away, but stayed on smiling vacantly and looking at his fingers. I think he had a sneaking liking for me, as had I for him. And thinking of Lewis, at last I said: "There won't be any of the first lot left by the time this is over. We joined too soon."

He answered with a snort of appreciation. "Yes, it will be the hundredth battalion which comes back. And the girls will hooray and the papers will talk about heroes, and it will be forgotten we ever went." He waved the flies from his face, and then he said: "Well, you understand about Lewis?" And away he went.

I sat down again and dozed as before. Norris

did not turn up for a long while, and I had no quarrel against him on that score. It was between ten and eleven when he and the two stretcher-bearers came climbing up the hill. The sun was high up, and very threatening. Sands sent the party to me, and they came and dropped on to the ground to pant and perspire. Then we lit cigarettes, and smoked a little while and talked wearily. I exchanged my news for theirs, and at the finish of the cigarettes I said: "How about it now?" Norris said, "Right-o," and the other men picked up the stretcher. We started to climb the hill.

The mail had arrived, and half-way up men sorted a heap of bags, and all with nothing to do loafed round on the chance of spotting something of their own. Letters were the one interest remaining to this drooping army. A good or bad mail made or marred a fellow's temper for the week. This collection was for the infantry, and we passed it by without interest. We climbed past the Infantry Headquarters, and up the next pinch to the mouth of the communication trench where Lewis was said to be. The place was quite deserted, except for hosts of flies. The trench was high and narrow, with many turns, and safe enough from shrapnel fire. We tramped along, panting and perspiring, and presently came on the body of Lewis on its back on the ground, three parts covered over with sacks. Lying thus, it looked no different from a sleeping man, for all covered themselves after this manner for shade and to escape the flies. But the trench walls told the truth. For a dozen yards the brains of Lewis clung to them. They could be traced by the flies settled there. It was a sight sickening to see. And on the trench floor were pieces of scalp and bits of raw flesh.

We said nothing as we stopped, but we brushed the flies from our faces, and somebody put down the stretcher. Out came cigarettes. The heat and the stiffness of the hill forced a rest before beginning work. The stretcher-bearers sat on the stretcher. I settled opposite, and Norris crouched at the head of the body. The flies, which had been disturbed by our coming, settled again at their task. We were at the straightest part of the trench; it ran a dozen yards without a turning, and it was because of this the shell had found a way in. It was a chance in fifty—in a hundred; but the ballot had been against Lewis. Well, he had gone, and we had stayed behind to sweat and curse the flies.

The blue smoke of our cigarettes curled into the air, for there was no breeze to scatter it. The flies camped in black masses on the sacking, the sacking lay wearily over the corpse, and the boots and leggings poked from underneath. They were big boots: Lewis was a tall fellow, and his feet had not been the least part of him. There was a shovel near, and I got up and collected pieces of his head, and put them on the sacking by his body, and covered them over. I took care not to explore underneath the sack. I had no relish for what might be there.

So this was the end of Lewis, the beloved of

his family, the fellow whose face had been the face of a girl. The golden hair was blotted with blood and dirt, and the worms were to make a bridal chamber of the sockets which had held his blue eyes. Presently there would be tears shed for him when the news went home, but he himself needed no pity. He had done his guard, and now he was off duty till Gabriel's réveillé. Our cigarettes ended at the same time.

"What about it?" Norris said to the others.

"Right-o!" And the four of us got to our feet. I spoke next.

"I'll give you a hand as far as the valley."

We spread out the stretcher, and laid on it the body. This was done without moving the sack. A last search was made for remains that might have escaped us. And then began the tiresome journey to the beach.

We had stirred up a regular hornet's nest, and we had ourselves to blame. The colonel had said: "If you hit a man right and hit him left, and then kick him in the behind, he is generally too surprised to do anything. That's our stunt for this afternoon." And so we had fixed up this little show. Our three batteries, two Scottish howitzer batteries and a New Zealand battery, were agreed to engage the enemy at the same moment. Directly he opened his mouth for the afternoon battle we were to slap at him. We had extra ammunition to spend. The colonel was like a schoolboy on holiday. He invited a couple of infantrymen, and we went away to a new observing station connected by telephone with the old place. I sat by to take messages in case of emergency.

The battle had opened well. Their guns no more than sniped at us, and very soon we shut them up altogether. The colonel peered into his periscope and chuckled to himself. Then all of a sudden they woke up and answered with big shells along our first line of trenches. It was our turn to be surprised. Our laughter lost its hearty ring. Our little party, the engineers of this business, had chosen a safe place for the present; but matters looked uncomfortable to the left hand, and the blameless infantry suffered. I sat by the colonel's feet, gathering how matters went from his brief remarks, from the explosions, and from the voices of our own shells tearing overhead. To and fro before me men pushed past on some duty or other, with lively faces and lively movements. The telephonist was crouched at my back, receiver strapped to his head. He repeated the colonel's orders in monotonous voice, and called out the replies. I was sleeping partner in the fight. I crossed my legs and put my chin in the cup of my hand, waiting what might happen. The colonel's face was crimson from the sun and from his feelings. Something was going wrong, for he was losing patience. He shifted from one leg to the other and frowned, and stared through the periscope, and snapped out orders at the telephonist. Just now I took the cigarette from my mouth, and looked at it. It was half-smoked.

"Why have the New Zealanders shut up shop?"

the colonel burst out. "What's happened to them? Find out from Mr. Sands what's happened to them!"

The telephonist buzzed the call, but got no answer. He buzzed again with like result. Alternately he buzzed and called for the next minute. Then he said: "Can't raise them, sir." The colonel was too busy to hear, and he went on calling.

"Have you got that through?" said the colonel, all of a sudden.

"No, sir. Can't raise them."

"What's up?"

"Don't know, sir. The line must be cut."

"Oh, damn!" The colonel chewed his top lip. "Are you there, Lake?"

"Yes, sir." I got up.

"Go along to Mr. Sands, and ask what's happened to the New Zealanders. Tell him the line is cut, and he must send someone along to mend it at once. Hurry, man, there's no time to lose!"

I knocked the ash from my cigarette, and put the butt into my mouth. Then I turned to the left hand and hurried along the trench. Almost at once I passed the traverse corner, and the group I had left were lost to sight.

I went at a trot wherever the trench was empty, but this was seldom, as much of the way the men were wide awake and in places they stood to arms. There was anxiety on most faces. Usually I progressed at a fast walk; but there were times when I must elbow the way forward. The fellows talked hard to one another, and those who knew me for an artilleryman called out to know what we were up to. In good truth I was advancing into the danger zone; the roar of the bursting shells was more terrible, and there were frequent marks of damage. All at once I came on a wrecked machine-gun emplacement where a shell had come in. The spot suggested the passage of an earthquake, and drops of blood were spilled about in plenty. Two men dug feverishly into the upheaved earth, and I saw the legs of a buried body sticking out. A dead man lay farther down the trench where he had been carried. He was plastered over with earth, his eyes and mouth were filled up with it. I pushed past the gathering. One of the diggers called after me, "The parapet's down there, mate. Look slick as you pass the open bit. The snipers are watching it." I waved a hand to show I heard.

I dodged by the open bit, and true enough two bullets chipped the earth behind me. There seemed no shrapnel falling; but that was of little account, the trenches were deep and safe enough for small stuff. But these big howitzer shells were a different matter. Nothing was proof against them. When one roared down in the neighbourhood, tearing to pieces everything, the heart to fight left a man. It was war more fitting gods. As I went along the pace shortened up my breath. I came on another dead man laid on his back, and had to manœuvre to pass without treading on him. I puffed at the cigarette end, for it was the last of the week's issue. It tasted what it was—cheap and nasty. As half the journey was done, I heard the scream of a shell right atop of me: there was a thud and then a dull roar which made my ears sing again, and the parapet a few yards distant crashed in. The ground broke into a trembling, and a dead man was thrown face up at my very feet. There came another scream hard atop of the first: another thud, another roar, so that my head buzzed again; the parapet nearer at hand toppled down, and the earth, flooding up, trapped me round the ankles. The ground shook to its centre, and I swear the dead man clapped his hands. I could have called out in sudden terror. I kept my head and kicked myself free, jumped over the dead man, and clambered across the mound of earth. Just then there was a noise of footsteps, and three men with white, twitching faces ran up. I warrant they thought the devil was at their heels. The sight of them pulled me together. I put my arms on either side of the trench and faced them coldly. The leading man was forced to come to a standstill. I said a few things to them, and from the way I spoke they took me for an officer; and in ten seconds I had them scuttling back to their posts like the cowardly hounds they were. I ran on again.

Sands leaned from his funk-hole in a very bored manner. "Message, sir, from the C.O.!" I called out. "Please find out why New Zealand Battery has ceased fire." Great sadness came into Sands's face: he nodded his head to himself. "Lake," he said, "you are too slow to be in time for your own funeral. I got that message two minutes ago over the 'phone."

I sat down to get back breath. The butt of the cigarette was in my lips, and I spat it out. The whole affair had taken place in the smoking of a cigarette end.

The summer wore on and came to its height. All day long the sun stared from a cloudless sky on to the baked earth. The midday heat was so fierce that the flies died. Dysentery and typhus took hold in earnest of the army. The hours were so many, it seemed the day would never end; the days were so many, it seemed the summer must last for ever. Men woke in the morning with the languor of despair. Even the zest for our evening battle left us: days passed when the enemy went to bed in peace. Instead of fighting, the colonel vanished to the dug-out of a friend, and left me to stare over the desolate debatable land and watch for the flash of guns. A keen haze shivered above the empty spaces, until the sun touched the horizon edge in the form of a crimson ball. That was the signal for the return home.

To be truthful, the nights were kinder than the days, and at sunset an evening breeze moved from the sea. So one gathered energy for the morrow. Often I sat on the balcony of my funk-hole, staring into the eye of the setting sun. Many lovely sunsets have I watched spread over the bay, and have fed on them my starved eyes. Next the sky faded, the sea grew dim and shadowy, and overhead stars came out. The cool of night moved abroad. It was drink to a thirsting man. The valley grew hushed, as now the armies forgot to fire at night. Or may be sudden alarm woke the echoes. Star shells scattered in the sky, a burst of rapid fire broke from the trenches, and sometimes our guns opened their mouths, and sent shells moving through the dark like red-hot cinders. But more often, as I have said, a hush fell on the valley. Most nights the fellows came over for a visit. It was the hour when men sucked at their pipes and opened their hearts. Many a strange love story was told under the eyes of the waiting stars. You saw the red glow of the cigarettes and pipes, and a face lit up for a moment. And after the stories—as silently as they arrived—the men went off to their dug-outs. It remained for me to unroll blankets and waterproof sheets, to undress and lie down. And sooner or later care was forgotten in sleep.

In the course of time the enemy received considerable reinforcements of big guns and ammunition, and while the papers were declaring Turkey was on the verge of collapse, our trenches were knocked atop of us in right good style.

The last time I saw Sands, he wandered over at sunset to squat down by my dug-out. He had done this same thing once or twice before: the habit was growing on him. May be melancholy had overcome at last his imperturbable spirit. We sat side by side staring at the sea. This evening my visitor was strangely depressed.

"Lake," he said, "what do you think of it?"

I shrugged my shoulders. When he got no answer he turned his head, and, our eyes meeting, he laughed. It was one of his short choky affairs. That ended our conversation. A great many fellows were going down to the sea with towels about their necks, and I wanted to join them. But Sands sat where he was, and I must wait for him to make a move. I spoke next.

"Their artillery is too much of a good thing now: it's over the odds being plugged at with six- and eight-inch shells. There ought to be a rule, nothing bigger than three-inch allowed, anyhow from the other side." He chuckled. I went on. "A fellow's not safe anywhere. A man has got to sit and chance having the whole place blown in on him. It comes hard on a fellow's nerves waiting to be blown up. You have a bad time every night where you are. It's the worst place in the line."

"Yes," Sands said, "it's pretty unhealthy about five o'clock. They have got our range properly. This evening they started to lob six-inch shells beside me. I had been relieved, but I thought I would see how many I could stand. I waited for three, and then I left. The next one came into the observing station, and blew the place to blazes. It was as well I had shifted." He gave a series of chuckles.

Soon afterwards he went off, and I picked up a towel and joined the throng moving to the beach. Half the army bathed at sundown, and on the way home men lined up and filled water-bottles for the next day. About sunset hour the beach was filled with naked men treading over the treacherous pebbles to the water, and with others drying and dressing. The piers overflowed divers, and the waves were dotted with the heads of swimmers, and there was more laughter and shouting than through all the rest of the day. But a false note jarred this harmony. Day and night waited Beachy Bill with devilish patience. There would come a whistle, a bang, and a great spluttering on the waves or woodwork of the piers, and the divers raced for cover, and the swimmers struck out for land. Beneath the cliffs men looked into each other's eyes and laughed nervously. And may be rose the cry for stretcher-bearers.

At breakfast-time one morning a man gathering firewood climbed too high up the opposite hill. We watched him, saying he took a risk. A sniper's bullet hit him through the chest, and he began to roll down the hill, and as he rolled he screamed like a wounded hare. I never heard a man scream that way before. He was tangled up in a root before he had rolled many yards, and then the stretcher-bearers took charge. I don't know what became of him; but my appetite for breakfast had lost its edge.

I was scratched myself about this time. I sat at sunset in the dug-out yarning with one of the fellows. The enemy shelled us in a happy-go-lucky way, and a piece of casing from a high-explosive shell grazed me on the side of the head. I came off with a headache and a little blood drawn; but it was a close touch.

Summer wore on. We on the Peninsula seemed no nearer victory; and the news from France and Russia was depressing. This was the time of the Russian retreat. Wisely, we were given good and bad news impartially, which made us believe the good news when it arrived. The information came by Reuter's telegrams, which were posted daily on the biscuit boxes by the beach and on notice boards at different headquarters. Men coming down to fill water-bottles, or to bathe, crowded the announcements and read with brief comment. The reading over, they cursed the heat, the flies, and their misfortunes, and tramped uphill again. There was no heart in affairs. The old fierceness had left the enemy equally with ourselves. At long intervals one or other goaded himself into wrath; but more generally there were to be heard only the crack of snipers' bullets, and the occasional voice of a gun.

Then were born some more rumours of reinforcements and a fresh advance; and there seemed truth in the matter when ammunition and guns appeared. Batteries of five-inch and six-inch howitzers arrived, and with them came barge loads of shells. Provision depots were formed in sheltered places in anticipation of the reinforcements. A gleam of hope lit the future.

Says the colonel to me one day as we pass the fork where Shrapnel and Monash Valleys join—"I can send you down to the Column as acting bombardier."

"Sir," I answer, "acting bombardier is a thankless job. The men know an acting bombardier draws no extra pay, and they value him accordingly."

"Well," says the colonel, "a man has got to make a beginning."

That is all our speech, but next day I am ordered down to the Column, and I go as full bombardier.

CHAPTER XIX

THE LAST OF ANZAC

The Column had dug themselves in on the ruins of our old headquarters. They were handy to the beach, and boasted an uninterrupted view of the sea. The place had much to recommend it; but it suffered from the attentions of Beachy Bill and his comrade of Anafarta. As a new-comer, I had poor choice of funk-holes; but I picked one in a hollow, screened from Beachy Bill and moderately protected from the Anafarta gun. Here I laid my kit and waited what might be in store.

I was growing ill. I had suffered long from dysentery, but that was in common with all the army. Now a terrible weariness took hold of me, with headache and bodily pains. I thought the attack would prove the affair of a day; but I could get no better. I wondered what was becoming of me.

I had no complaint to lodge on the score of duty. Two days after arrival, I was detailed three men and sent a little way up the valley to guard a provision depot built in anticipation of the reinforcements. These reinforcements now were expected daily. I divided the guard into shifts of two hours on duty and four hours off, and after seeing that the work was carried out, I could call my time my own. I put up an awning, and slept under its shadow through the heat of the day, in defiance of the searching odours of the yellow cheeses simmering in the sun. At five o'clock in the afternoon it was possible to move abroad, and about then the enemy put in a few rounds of some ancient field-piece, half cannon and half trench mortar. It hurled a rough iron ball which shattered into three or four pieces. The provision stack seemed always the target. And visiting Taubes commonly left a card in the shape of a bomb. Several stretcher-parties started from our neighbourhood on the journey to the beach, but the provision stack and its guard remained. But, as I hint, if nothing demanded your stay, it was as well about five o'clock to visit other parts.

Thus, between five and six o'clock, I took such of our water-bottles as wanted filling, and started towards the beach. The first of the bathers were coming down, and most of them carried empty water-bottles slung round their shoulders. Below the junction of Monash and Shrapnel Valleys began a wide deeply-cut road, driven by the sappers in earlier days. On the left hand was a considerable fenced cemetery, full of cared-for graves. As afternoon declined, this sheltered road became crowded with passengers. At the end of twenty or thirty yards it emptied on to a hillock overlooking the sea. Here was a square of ground quite destitute of cover from shell-fire. The path ran round it, and by a flight of steps led you down on to the beach.

The ocean was always blue and always calm; but it was emptier than of yore. The transports long since had steamed away, and enemy submarines had scared the main body of the fleet. Commonly a monitor waited there, and a number of destroyers; and these were all the craft of battle. But in shore, round about the jetties, was much movement. All day arrived barges of provisions and ammunition, and if you waited long and watched carefully, you might welcome a battery of guns. And many barges were anchored at hand, waiting their turn. Also there were the pinnaces bearing the wounded to the hospital ship, The army medical men had a jetty of their own. decorated with a Red Cross flag, at the foot of the road I have spoken about: the other jetties overflowed men bearing provisions and ammunition from the barges, or pumping up the fresh water. And at sunset these workers were exchanged for scores of naked bathers.

Always there was something to interest you on the beach, be it Reuter's telegrams, or the chance meeting of acquaintances, or the sight of other men working while you loafed. Then there was the delightful uncertainty of Beachy Bill. You remembered him most acutely while waiting in a long queue of men to fill your water-bottle. The sun blazed on you, and you thought of Beachy Bill and his ill-humours. Water-tanks were his favourite targets.

Beachy Bill had no call to be careful of his mark; did he miss one target, he found another. There were stacks of provisions larger than houses. There were stores of fodder. There were the hospitals and the headquarters of the generals. There were the baker shops, the butcher shops, the cobblers, the workshops, the post offices, and such places. Also from end to end the beach was crowded with soldiers and mules, and blocked with a hundred matters of value. One met many sounds and smells; and to the last the pebbles sank underfoot. No amount of passage stamped them flat. At the farther end of the beach, better protected from enemy fire, were in building the vast ammunition reserves; and guns and their waggons accumulated here for the expected advance. It seemed the colonel's dream—ammunition to burn—must find realisation.

Seldom I went farther than the Australian post office, where I had acquaintances; and my visits were paid at tea-time. In the same neighbourhood was a wire enclosure, where were kept prisoners of war until such time as they could be shipped away. Those I saw were shabby, depressed creatures; and the hair and beards of many were streaked with grey. Yet our own appearance could scarcely have been better. The prisoners had put up what shelter was possible, and they sat and dozed in it all day, and at evening wandered round the enclosure with morose looks.

The shadow of Death over the land did not prevent certain spirits from seeking to turn an honest or dishonest penny. A trade began in eggs, chocolate, tinned fish and cigarettes, smuggled over from Imbros and elsewhere. Profits made were three and four hundred per cent. Eggs at four and five shillings the dozen were sold out at once. I have been abroad at four in the morning to be in time. The traffic was stopped by order presently; but you might still find what you wanted did you know where to go.

My guard duty at the provision depot continued for the better part of a fortnight, and during that time considerable preparations for our attack were made. Batteries arrived ashore, including a number of howitzer batteries. Some of them were concealed among the gullies running from the sea, others were parked for the present on the beach. Men unloaded shells until it seemed we never could fire the total. We had a hard nut to crack; but this time it appeared we would be given the nutcrackers. Presently the first of the reinforcements appeared on the scene. Those I saw—and I saw thousands—were newly formed battalions showing over many youthful faces. I could not lose the feeling that we needed sterner material. However, there came good Indian regiments—Sikhs and Gurkas I recognised. The Englishmen dug themselves in in all unoccupied places. The valleys filled with them. We were quick to experience the change of numbers; henceforward the filling of water-bottles was a bitter business. Three or four days must be spent before the attack, and the Englishmen had no luck in that time. The big shells fired by the enemy haphazard into the valleys found targets on many occasions. This cold-blooded sitting-about to be blown up must have tried severely new nerves.

When the Englishmen arrived, my guard on the stores ended. An officer turned up at dark one evening and took over the place. I was neither glad nor sorry at the change: I dismissed my men, rolled my blankets, and went back to the Column. To tell the truth, ill-health had brought me to the end of my tether. Strength was leaving me: it was hard work now to walk uphill; I could not travel far without resting. At morning I did not know how I should last through the day.

The night following my return to the Column was passed dragging a battery of heavy guns from the beach into position on our left flank. The work went forward in the dark, with no more than the occasional light of a lantern. We moved the guns by means of ropes, men in long lines toiling at the work. The sea, lit dimly by chilly stars, moved on our left hand, throwing the little waves upon the pebbles with the sound of rustling leaves. All the distance of our journey, the beach was busy with men at final preparations. Batteries of guns moved to this and that position; long lines of men bore after them ammunition. In quiet places we passed drafts from Indian regiments. Brief commands and the jangle of arms came to us. Such parties as I describe were engaged on their own business, and said no word to us, nor took we account of them. There was endless mutter of rifle-fire from the trenches, and other sounds were the rustling of the wavelets and the mumble of the guns rolling over the sand. In early morning hours the battery was in position; but much was to do. It must be hid from aircraft. Greenery was scarce in the neighbourhood, and tough to cut when found. That we might not sleep over our duty, at intervals shells fired at random hurled by us and burst with blinding flashes, and star shells climbed into the sky. Dawn moved vaguely in the heavens as we turned home.

Twelve hours later the attack had begun, and our batteries were heavily engaged. By evening the fury of both armies was terrible. Shells of all weights descended upon us. And the fierceness of our replies can have been no whit less, for the big reserve of shells attacked by the guns threatened exhaustion, and a call came for further supplies. The Column worked themselves to a standstill that night: neither, I warrant you, was their work a coward's work. A man carried on either shoulder a live eighteen-pounder shell. As you left the A Battery trenches to cross the open space to the Pimple, the country seemed ploughed by a giant's plough. It was hard to be sure of things in the dark; but all standing objects appeared swept from the scene. Dead men gaped at you wherever shadows were least thick. When I arrived the fury of the Turkish fire had abated for a while, but even so it was not a journey one would wish to repeat. However, my first journey was my last. The climb up the hills and the weight of the shells stole my strength. I fell down half a dozen times on the journey, and though I managed the return empty-handed, I could reach my funk-hole and do no more than that. I went to sleep with the gun-fire knocking at my ears.

And the sound heard last at night woke me in the morning. It was even more terrible than before, so that I looked to sea, and there found the ocean filled again with a great fleet. The guns of the battleships bellowed with the voices of olden days. Verily we must succeed this time, was my thought. It was early yet, though the day was quite light. I found I could scarcely raise my head. A fever burnt me; and my strength seemed all gone. I lay back again among the blankets. Ever and anon the guns at sea ceased fire, and then I discovered the army still was heavily engaged. Again and again broke out the fierce voices of field-guns, and the musketry rolled up and down tirelessly. The enemy replied with fully as much spirit; but the beach bore most part of their fury. Continually the walls of my funk-hole vibrated.

Strength returned somewhat while I lay there; but I continued to feel most miserable. Presently I pulled clothes on and made breakfast. I drank a little; but I could not eat. Then I joined the other fellows, and together we watched the battle. I was not on duty before nightfall, and the day was my own. The enemy fire continued with great fury, and kept us on the threshold of our funk-holes; but in the afternoon I went down to the tanks to fill a water-bottle, and to see anything worth seeing.

Below my funk-hole, where the road ran by the bottom of the hill, was a small shed used as a mortuary. Stretcher-bearers coming from the valley immediately to the right hand left their burdens here. Most days you would find three or four blanketed forms on the floor, and sometimes the number was greater. You might guess at the enemy shell-fire by what was to be found here. To-day as I passed on the way to the beach, fifteen or sixteen bodies lay there in two rows, and a party of men had arrived for the burial. On my return the shed had filled again.

Near General Headquarters I saw a strange happening. Four men carried a single man who struggled and shouted, and they found their work no easy matter. At first I thought fear had sent him mad, later I discovered him to be drunk. The party marched slowly, with many pauses for struggle. They moved in the direction of the cells. It was no pleasant sight to come on at an hour when every man was needed.

I made what inquiries of the attack I could; but gleaned no news of value. Our success was enormous, I heard. The Englishmen had gained a great bite of country round Suvla Bay. Numbers of prisoners were arriving under escort of Indians, and that might be a fact to judge by. Round the hospitals were countless wounded, and many hospital ships waited at sea. Filling my water-bottle, I returned to the Column. The assault continued all day; but it abated towards evening.

About sunset the sergeant-major sent for me to say I must report at Brigade Headquarters. I made tea at once, and afterwards rolled together blankets and kit and prepared for the march. So little strength remained to me, I had difficulty in lifting the bundle to my shoulder. I began my journey under the light of the stars.

By this time a great stillness had fallen over the land. The artillery of both sides had shut their mouths. The musketry still rolled from end to end of the trenches; but the sound was so even, and my ears so used to it, that scarcely I heard it. I climbed along the hillside as far as the cutting which joins Shrapnel Valley with the beach. The cutting took me to the valley foot. Where the two valleys join, I sat down for a first rest. There was a cross at the back of me, marking a grave much grown over with scrub. It was the grave of a B Battery corporal I had known well. I found myself wishing we might change places. It seemed impossible to climb the rest of the way up the hill. I wondered what was becoming of me.

The valley was very empty, which may have accounted in part for its stillness. The majority of the Englishmen had been taken for the attack on Suvla Bay, and those of our own infantry not in the trenches lay low in the hills on either side, mistrustful no doubt of a second bombardment. I saw the gleam of a few fires, and even heard voices of men. Presently I got again to my feet.

I went along the empty valley, meeting only a

mule waggon on the way. As I arrived at the waterbutts, two star-shells burst in the sky, and a volley of rapid fire broke from the trenches. But at the end of a little while the fire died again to an even roll. I rested a second time at the foot of the hill where Headquarters was dug in, and then began the last bitter pinch. I thought I should never reach the top; but I scrambled there at last. Before reporting to the sergeant-major, I sat down to get breath.

The night was dark, but I was used to it. Round about me the men sat at the mouths of their funk-holes, talking together and smoking and dreaming. The colonel, with a couple of other men, was in the officers' dug-out: he spoke down the 'phone, relating the day's events so far as I heard. I looked for the sergeant-major, and found him in his dug-out, lying on the blankets. He looked tired and ill. A candle in a cigarette tin lit the place. I put down my head, for the roof was low, and peered inside.

"I've come to report myself, sergeant-major." He looked at me over the candle and blinked his eyes: I was in shadow and he took a moment to recognise me.

"Oh, it's you, Lake. You'll be wanted in the morning for observing. You brought your kit, I suppose?"

I said "Yes," and then "Good-night," and went across to the telephone office.

There I found Wilkinson. He read *The Bulletin* by the light of a lantern. The receiver was strapped over his ears. He seemed pleased to see me, and said all of a sudden, "You look crook."

"I feel pretty crook," I answered. And then I sat down and asked for the news. Wilkinson had plenty to give.

"They've got Lonesome Pine," he exclaimed.

"By Jove!" I said. "What about the Jolly?"

"They've not got that yet. They found tons of ammunition in the Lonesome Pine trenches; and there's a report through that our fellows and the Gurkas have taken '971.' It sounds dinkum." His speech was excited. He told me a lot more, all as hopeful.

"I feel pretty crook," I said in the end. "I think I'll turn in." He gave me a long look and nodded good-night, and I went outside to look for a funk-hole. I ran into Woods, who suggested I should sleep with him. I spread out my blankets by him and lay down, hoping I might not wake again.

"Take this stretcher case," said the man on the jetty to the man on the barge. I was lifted up again. There was a pause while they manœuvred me from jetty to barge, and then I was laid down among the others. My eyes opened with effort. I lay between two Indians. He on the right was without motion, with a pallor about his face warning of Death's coming; the other sat cross-legged and bent over me when my eyes opened. He said many words in a high cooing voice; but I understood only Australia.

He meant to be of comfort, he pulled about the blanket beneath my head that I might rest the easier. Over all the wide deck lay bodies of broken men. Drawn faces with shut eyes were turned up to the sky. The deck was dirty with loose straws and other rubbish, for the barge had been claimed in a hurry for this new use.

They carried me on among the last; the deck was filled; there came the bustle of casting off; the pinnace that would tow us tugged at her cables; we moved from shore. Again my eyes closed. The afternoon sun beat on my face; but a breeze from the ocean spoiled its fury. The cries from shore died; but plainly yet I heard the musketry tattoo. It had come over the waters to meet me four months before; it came over the waters after me as I floated away. The barge moved on the calm seas with easy lulling motion, and fain I would have slept. But I must open my eyes to see the last of Anzac. As we drew away it was discovered from end to end—tall bare hills pocked over with dug-outs: a wonderful, unforgettable scene painted in browns and smoky greys. What brave hopes tumbled there, what high courage spent, what rich blood spilt, what old hearts broken! Amen. Amen. And as I shut my eyes, Beachy Bill fired at us a salute.

My eyes opened yet again. The barge was at a standstill, and there were sounds of raised voices. We were under the shadow of a hospital ship. There came a rattling of chains, and followed it the work of lifting us aboard. Presently I mounted through the air. Arms came out to steady me and draw me in. And then I found myself looking into a woman's face.

And now—after the manner of signallers when their message ends—I write

VIK E.

www.ingramcontent.com/pod-product-compliance
Ingram Content Group UK Ltd.
Pitfield, Milton Keynes, MK11 3LW, UK
UKHW041952190726
13854UKWH00005B/1925

9 781845 749224